VICTORIA
& ALBERT

VICTORIA
& ALBERT

A Royal Love Affair

SARA SHERIDAN
WITH DAISY GOODWIN

HarperCollins*Publishers*

CONTENTS

INTRODUCTION

I T COULD HAVE been a disaster. First cousins catapulted into a match that suited the dynastic ambitions of their relatives. A pair who seemed to have nothing in common: he was a highbrow who had studied science and philosophy; she liked dancing and watching lion tamers. He got up early and ate very frugally; she liked to sleep in and loved tucking into a plate of lamb chops. All they had in common was their liking for dogs (he had a greyhound called Eos; she, of course, had Dash, her Cavalier King Charles spaniel), music – oh, and an overwhelming physical attraction for each other.

You only have to read Victoria's diaries during their courtship to know that this is no marriage of convenience but a throbbingly passionate love match. She writes about Albert in his white cashmere breeches with nothing underneath; he writes about how his whole soul longs for Victoria. This was a pair who couldn't keep their hands off each other, as their nine children in seventeen years testifies. One of my favourite facts about Albert is that he came up with a special gadget that meant he could lock their door without getting out of bed, which was handy if you had a palace full of servants and children. But Victoria and Albert's marriage was passionate in every sense. They were the Elizabeth Taylor and Richard Burton of the nineteenth century – two huge personalities

who were locked in a battle for mastery over the other. They fought fiercely, with stand-up rows that raged all over the palace, and then they made up with equal passion. Their rows were over things that many modern couples can relate to: the upbringing of their children, the amount of time they spent away from each other, the inequality between them when it came to status – as Albert wrote sadly to one of his friends, 'I am the husband but not the master in the house.'

However, unlike some modern mismatched royal couples we could mention, Victoria and Albert were able to accommodate this, allowing Albert to make a significant contribution to his adopted country, while still supporting his wife. After his death at the age of forty-two, Victoria wrote that Albert did everything for her, even chose her bonnets, but I think she was trying in retrospect to portray herself as the kind of perfect submissive Victorian wife that she most definitely wasn't. One of the things that makes Victoria such an attractive subject for a modern writer and audience is that no one ever puts her in a corner. She may have liked to present herself as a little woman – and she was undoubtedly small – but she never, ever went under. The pictures of the couple always have Victoria gazing adoringly up at her husband, but that was definitely her way of redressing the imbalance in their relationship. As I have Victoria say in a scene in the first episode of series two, when Albert is dressed up in his Hussar's uniform, ready to inspect his regiment, 'It may be your regiment, Albert, but it is my army.'

Despite the dramatic nature of their fights (the hairbrush-throwing incident in the series and the time when Albert refuses to come back from a dinner are both based on real events), Victoria and Albert were brilliant at keeping their domestic squabbles out of the public eye. After a succession of fat old kings with frumpy

German wives, the young Victoria, her handsome prince and their ever-growing brood of adorable children were an image that gladdened the nation's heart – or at least the part of the nation that wasn't complaining about how much all this domestic bliss was costing. In the 1840s the royal family became, for the first time, not just a symbol of power, but also a role model. Everybody wanted to play happy families like the royal couple, who unlike their predecessors did not have lovers or indulge in gambling or other decadent pursuits. Victoria and Albert may have given each other lavish presents in private, but in public they seemed like an ordinary bourgeois couple, just with better clothes. Their genius as a couple was not just to have one of the most successful royal marriages ever, but to reinvent the British monarchy as a cosy incarnation of domestic bliss that everyone could aspire to. Inside the palace their fights may have been rocket-fuelled, but in the public gaze they were a model of serenity.

Their success at projecting themselves as the perfect couple has meant that the real drama behind Victoria and Albert's marriage has been largely forgotten, an oversight which I hope to put right in the series and in this book. It's important to know how hard they had to work on their marriage as the problems they faced were those that will resonate with many people today, even if they did have a lot more money and help and much better jewellery. Victoria and Albert inspired a nation in the nineteenth century. They can still inspire us today.

~DAISY GOODWIN, SCREENWRITER OF *VICTORIA*

FACT & FICTION

The great joy for me about writing *Victoria* is that I am never lost for inspiration. The place I start is always the diaries, not so much for a factual record of her life, but to get that unmistakable tone of voice – observant, emphatic, passionate. In the diaries and letters that are in Victoria's own hand (most of the diaries were transcribed after her death by her younger daughter, Beatrice), you can actually see her state of mind – the pages are full of CAPITAL LETTERS and emphatic underlining, and after Albert's death you can see the grief in her letters in the way that her usually beautiful script degenerates into an inchoate scrawl.

But while I am inspired by the diaries, they are not Holy Writ; indeed, they are only reliable as an indication of Victoria's state of mind, and sometimes not even that, as her diaries were only semi-private – in the early years they were read by both her mother and Baroness Lehzen, and I am sure that Albert might have glanced through them during their marriage, too. She doesn't, for example, ever write about her rows with Albert, even though we know from contemporary accounts that their relationship was not a bed of roses. A woman who habitually describes her husband as an angel is to my mind protesting a

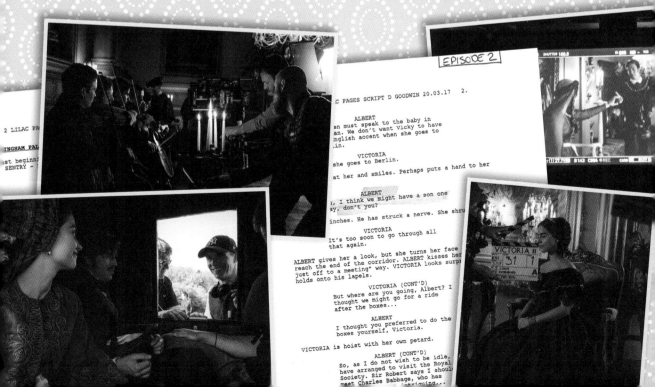

little too much. My guess is that after a particularly stormy row with Albert, Victoria would assuage her guilt by writing about him in particularly glowing terms. Her diaries are rather like the carefully staged portraits of the royal couple in which Albert sits down casually while Victoria stands beside him, all wifely attention. The truth of the matter is that no one, not even Albert, could sit in the Queen's presence without her permission, so there is nothing natural about his pose.

Although I was trained as a historian, when I am writing *Victoria* I approach the material as a dramatist; my historical training means that I know what the parameters of credibility are, but it is my fictional empathy that allows me to put words into my characters' mouths that are emotionally true. There are some people who have taken exception to the way I portrayed the relationship between the teenage Victoria and her first prime minister, Lord Melbourne, claiming there could never have been such an intense romantic bond between monarch and minister (there are also many more people who wish that I had disregarded history entirely and made that bond even more intense – there is some steamy Vicbourne fan fiction out there), but while Victoria probably didn't go to Brocket Hall to propose to Lord M, as I had her do in series one, there is no doubt that she was as smitten with him as a teenage girl can be and he felt the same way about her. A contemporary diarist who served as Clerk to the Privy Council, Charles Greville, called Victoria's infatuation with Melbourne 'sexual if she but knew it', and Melbourne was a man with a great capacity for love. The scene at Brocket Hall is fictional, but the emotions behind it are not, and I can confirm

that Melbourne was indeed captivated by rooks, which do mate for life.

One of the strange things about writing *Victoria* is that the real events are always harder to believe than anything I could imagine. The story of the Boy Jones (see pages 262–63), a teenage boy who managed to wander in and out of Buckingham Palace seemingly at will, despite being caught twice, is extraordinary but completely true. Today we expect our rulers to be surrounded by a security detail, but access to Victoria was remarkably easy by today's standards – over the course of her reign there were no less than seven attempts on her life. She was a very tempting target for young men who wanted to make their mark on the world, if not necessarily on the Queen – in the first three attempts, after all, the weapons were not loaded.

Another of my secret weapons is to read the newspapers from the year I am writing about – it helps me to write in the present, instead of always with the benefit of hindsight. We know that Victoria had nine healthy children, but at a time when childbirth was the biggest cause of female mortality you have to read the papers of the time to understand how the nation must have held its breath each time the Queen went into labour. When I wrote the Christmas episode for the second series I included a scene where Albert falls into a frozen lake at Buckingham Palace and has to be rescued by Victoria. Everyone liked the script but there was a feeling that I might have gone too far with the rescue scene – it was just too dramatically neat. It was with a certain amount of schadenfreude that I was able to produce the newspaper report of this actual event. When it comes to Victoria and Albert, it seems you really can't make it up.

CHAPTER 1
MODERN ROYALS

*'Great events make me quiet and calm;
it is only trifles that irritate my nerves.'*

···· LETTER FROM VICTORIA TO LEOPOLD,
KING OF THE BELGIANS, 4 APRIL 1848 ····

IN THE WINTER OF 1840 at Buckingham Palace, only a few weeks after the 21-year-old Queen Victoria had given birth to her first daughter, Victoria ('Vicky'), the Queen was taking tea by the open fire with her husband, Prince Albert, and some of her ladies-in-waiting. It was clear that Victoria was upset; there were red patches on her cheeks and her eyes were glassy. Those in attendance knew that the couple had argued and the Queen had been crying, but nobody said a word about it. Victoria had a temper and was prone to outbursts, so her ladies were used to treading on eggshells to avoid getting on the wrong side of her.

Suddenly, overcome by fury, Victoria snapped. Eyes blazing, she took up her cup and threw the hot tea all over her husband. Albert sprang from his chair. 'What do you think of that?' he said irritably, drying his face with a handkerchief. The tea had stained his silk cravat and jacket – he was lucky not to have been burned. Albert never rose to his wife's temper tantrums and, instead, he stalked out of the room. This did nothing to alleviate Victoria's anger and left her ladies squirming with discomfort.

VICTORIA:
I just remembered
how awful it was, at
Kensington. I never
knew what it meant
to be happy.

MELBOURNE:
But you knew it
was possible.

VICTORIA:
I always knew that
I would make my
own way, one day.

....
Above: Victoria's infamous uncle, George IV.

VICTORIA HAD ONLY just discovered that, even before her first child, the infant princess, had been christened, she was pregnant again. She hated the idea of being tied to 'breeding'. For a woman who had escaped a suffocating childhood and cast off her ambitious mother and her mother's insidious advisor, Sir John Conroy, to take the throne in her own right, child-bearing felt like a trap that took her away from the life she really wanted. As far as Victoria was concerned, it was too soon to get pregnant again and it felt desperately unfair. She clearly blamed Albert, and much preferred the challenges of ruling the country to the job of securing the succession.

'There never was an individual less regretted by his fellow creatures than this deceased king.'

~ THE TIMES ON THE DEATH OF GEORGE IV,
VICTORIA'S UNCLE, 16 JULY 1830

When Victoria came to the throne on 20 June 1837, the British royal family was not popular. The House of Hanover, of which she was the sixth successive monarch, was viewed as foreign and corrupt. There hadn't been a woman on the throne for more than a century – not since the death of Queen Anne in 1714 – and many questioned whether a woman as young as Victoria could do the job. At under five feet tall, she was tiny, didn't have the formidable presence of Elizabeth I, and had only inherited the throne because her many uncles had failed to produce a legitimate male heir.

VICTORIA THE FEMINIST?

Victoria did not believe in votes for women. She was furious with her daughter, Princess Alice, for supporting the suffragist cause. But then, if you are the most powerful woman in the world, you don't need the ballot box to make your voice heard. My feeling about Victoria is that while she liked to portray herself as a devoted wife, who left all the important stuff to her husband, this could not have been further from the truth. Victoria may have said that women were not suited to politics, but that didn't stop her from taking a view on (and some would say meddling in) the affairs of state for the whole

of her sixty-three years on the throne. Victoria may have looked up with submissive adoration at Albert in family photographs, but in reality she had strong views about everything. I particularly like the letter that she wrote to the Home Secretary in 1889 with her advice on the best way to catch Jack the Ripper: had he, she enquired, 'searched the seamen's hostels for bloody clothing?'

One of the most empowering aspects of Victoria's character for a modern woman is her total lack of guilt. As a working mother I have spent my entire working life agonising over

VICTORIA 2 - EP 1 PEACH PAGES SCRIPT DAISY GOODWI

PAGES SCRIPT DAISY GOODWIN 23.02.17 38.

LEOPOLD (CONT'D)
portant that it develops
t way.

ALBERT
htfully)
    marriage...

he whole party stops.

VICTORIA
er is not even twelve
! I think that when she is
e to marry she will have
deas.

LEOPOLD
dies have a mind of their
t is true. But sometimes -
oks significantly at
em)
lders know best.

ORIA is not amused.

LEOPOLD
(shrugs)
Afghanistan... I think, Albert,
that a young man of your abilities
should be able to take her mind of
such things.

ALBERT says nothing. Behind them, BUCCLEUCH
falls behind with EMMA. He looks at BUCCLEU

ERNEST
Lead us not into temptation.
(Emma smiles ruefully)
Will the Duchess of Sutherland b
coming to the christening, I
wonder?

He stops, unable to continue. EMMA takes

EMMA
Yes, Sir.
(beat)
With the Duke.

ERNEST looks away.

whether I was giving my children enough attention. Victoria was refreshingly free of this modern malaise. She was also wonderfully free from vanity; she loved good looks in others, but didn't spend hours in front of the mirror agonising about her own. Her fashion sense was idiosyncratic; when she visited France the courtiers laughed at the bag she carried around, which was embroidered with a golden poodle. It had been made for her by her daughter Vicky and Victoria didn't care what the French thought.

What makes Victoria so interesting is that instead of pretending to be a man like her celebrated predecessor Elizabeth I, who famously made a speech declaring that she had the 'body of a weak and feeble woman, but the heart and stomach of a king', Victoria found a way of ruling as a woman, not as a surrogate man. She did not don the Victorian equivalent of a power suit, but kept her bonnet on throughout her reign. Victoria showed the world that it was possible to be a wife, a mother and the most powerful woman in the

world. That is why, to me, she is the most surprising and inspiring heroine. Her position meant that she didn't have to wait for a man to make the first move – she proposed to Albert – and no man was allowed to interrupt her. And she loved sex. Victoria was fallible and often infuriating, but she never doubted her own worth. How many women can say the same?

THE QUEEN'S
DRESSER,
SKERRETT:
No one here will
have jewels like
yours, Ma'am.

AT FIRST VICTORIA had been seen as the 'bottom of the barrel' and there had been publicly aired concerns that she would never be able to manage the duties required. The young Queen had a lot to prove. Immediately issues were raised, including a royal family feud, when Victoria's uncle, Ernest, became King of Hanover and claimed that the Hanoverian Jewels were, in part, his inheritance. While this issue rumbled on, Victoria quickly established herself as queen, and in less than three years she had married, given birth and established herself as a competent political operator. But pregnancy took her away from public life and it also altered her fledgling relationship with her handsome new husband. Both of them were still finding their feet within the relationship and, indeed, at court.

THE
DIAMOND QUESTION

WHEN VICTORIA CAME to the throne of Great Britain she could not inherit the throne of Hanover, as the law in Germany excluded women from the succession. The two kingdoms were separated for the first time in 123 years when the Duke of Cumberland, Victoria's Uncle Ernest, was crowned King of Hanover. Ernest demanded a portion of the jewels in the royal collection as part of his inheritance – the monarchies had been invested in the same person for over a century so the jewels, he said, could not belong solely to the British Crown. But Victoria flatly refused, arguing that the collection had been bought with English money.

Ernest was furious and bitterly complained to a friend, 'I hear the little Queen is loaded with my diamonds, which made a very fine show.' The wrangling continued for years and a commission was appointed to investigate the matter. Victoria referred to the dispute as 'the diamond question', and even after King Ernest died in 1851 his son continued the claim until 1857 when the matter was finally settled and Victoria had to hand over some items to the Hanoverian Ambassador in London.

PRIMOGENITURE

PRIMOGENITURE IS THE CUSTOM or law of the first-born legitimate son inheriting the throne in preference to daughters or older illegitimate sons. According to this practice, a female member of a dynasty can only succeed to the throne if she has no living brothers and no deceased brothers with surviving legitimate descendants. A dynast's sons and their lines of descent all come before that dynast's daughters and their lines. Older sons and their lines come before younger sons and their lines. Older daughters and their lines come before younger daughters and their lines. Britain, unlike France, Russia and Hanover, did not have Salic law, which prevented women from inheriting the throne. Victoria's predecessor, William IV, had been King of Great Britain and Hanover. However, Victoria, as a woman, could not inherit the throne of Hanover, so the crown went to the male in succession – the Duke of Cumberland.

Victoria became the heir apparent upon the death of her father in 1820 for this very reason – she was his only child, and the uncles who were older than her father had no legitimate heirs who survived childhood, and although two of the younger uncles did have legitimate sons, Victoria's claim took precedence because her father was the next in line. It was a different story for Victoria's own daughter, of course. Princess Victoria, though the first-born of the Queen's nine children, was passed over in favour of her younger brother, Bertie, who became King Edward VII in 1901 on Victoria's death.

THE ALLIANCE VICTORIA had made with Albert was key to her success as monarch. The young couple were very much in love – Victoria wrote reams about Albert in her diary, sometimes multiple times a day. She idolised her handsome cousin and set down her happiness at their life together in the pages of her journal, sparing few details about the sexual nature of their relationship. 'We didn't sleep much,' she admitted smugly the morning after their wedding. Albert's style in his (less frequently kept) diary is less effusive, but in his letters to his wife he often declared his ardour, signing himself 'in body and soul ever your slave' in one of 1839.

The future of the monarchy rested on the shoulders of these two young people – still in their very early twenties – yet all was not entirely well at the start. Victoria was nervous at first of Albert encroaching on her position as Queen. The Prince declared he only wanted to help his wife undertake her duties, but Victoria didn't entirely trust him. On matters of state in the early days she often turned for advice to her first prime minister, Lord Melbourne (see pages 56–7), and to her childhood governess and confidante, Baroness Louise Lehzen (see pages 120–21), before consulting Albert, if she consulted him at all.

VICTORIA:
You couldn't beat me even with a head start.

ALBERT:
Maybe I know how happy it makes you to win, *Liebes*.

Opposite: Princess Victoria, the first-born of Queen Victoria's children, was passed over in favour of her younger brother, to become monarch. Left: The couple married at the Chapel Royal in St James's Palace.

JENNA COLEMAN
PLAYS
QUEEN VICTORIA

'Series Two gives us the opportunity to explore Victoria and Albert's early years – their honeymoon effectively. We see how Victoria learns to balance a marriage, motherhood and being Queen. How Albert copes with not being master of his own house. The tectonic plates of their marriage behind the scenes and in a political sphere are constantly shifting and leads to a thunderous clash of wills and a burning passionate fire between them.'

VICTORIA

'I'm trying to play this impulsive young girl that's full of passion and vitality squeezed into the role of queen ... She finds controlling herself difficult.'

···· JENNA COLEMAN (VICTORIA) ····

THE YEARS COVERED in the second series of *Victoria* were in some ways the heyday of Victoria's young life. She had broken free from the influence of her mother, escaped the confines of the Kensington System (the restrictive set of rules she had to live by as a child) and was starting married life with the man she loved. However, these years also had their challenges.

The loss of her beloved Lord Melbourne as prime minister in 1841 was difficult, and though Sir Robert Peel slowly proved himself a worthy replacement, she struggled to let go. Across Europe the old royal regimes were being challenged. While there were some gains in British military action, there were also losses, and as a national figurehead it was down to Victoria to maintain national pride and optimism.

Victoria's greatest challenge during this period, however, was undoubtedly that of motherhood. She bore four children in five years while also ruling the country.

Ultimately, Victoria came through with flying colours and the period can be seen as her coming of age and the years in which her marriage established itself. She was, above all else, a passionate young woman, discovering her own sexuality and exercising power over her world in a way that no other woman of the era could. Her achievement was to maintain a sound public face while enjoying the private family life she craved. As the constraints of her childhood fell away and with her young family established, the trials and tribulations of these years form the foundation of one of the longest and most successful reigns in British history.

VICTORIA:
Albert, Lehzen
said your father
was propositioning
one of the ballet
dancers last night.
He should go back
to Coburg.

THE TASK VICTORIA faced should not be underestimated. All across Europe, in the 1830s and 1840s, new philosophical movements were developing and in the early years of Victoria's reign there were huge social and political upheavals. The Chartist movement, which began with Victoria's reign, demanded universal suffrage, secret ballots and votes for women. The stage was set for rebellions Europe-wide by the end of the 1840s and in Britain it was no different. It's easy to forget the unpopularity of the monarchy in Victoria's early days on the throne and that on seven occasions there were attempts on her life. If Victoria wanted the British monarchy to survive, she would have to make changes to how it was viewed.

'It is worth being shot at – to see how much one is loved.'
~LETTER FROM VICTORIA TO HER ELDEST DAUGHTER, VICKY,
6 MARCH 1882

As her consort in this endeavour, Albert was a good choice. Victoria's uncles who had previously sat on the throne had been louche, lavish and egotistical. They were not loved or, indeed, widely respected. Together, Victoria and Albert quickly began to change the way British royalty presented itself, updating the public persona of the royal family and gradually winning supporters to their cause. Big decisions were taken on the comfortable sofas of their drawing rooms, but often the changes the young couple made were small. They were both shrewd publicists and well aware of the anti-German sentiment that had been levelled at the House of Hanover for more than a century, so while they spoke German in private, they stuck to English in public.

Their relationship became an important tool for Victoria – a young couple very much in love proved a great rallying point for public attention. She and Albert, despite early apparent differences in interests, grew to have a lot in common, both loving the open air, music, books, history and art, and they were almost unique as a royal couple in their loyalty to each other.

ENERATIONS OF PREDECESSORS in both of their families had been mired in infidelity and marital scandal, and the young couple's devotion was a breath of fresh air that left many subjects feeling inspired. Albert claimed to feel nauseous at the very thought of sex outside of marriage, and there is no doubt that the young Queen felt a huge physical pull towards her husband. She was passionate about him and referred to their time in bed as 'fun'.

The flipside of this, however, was her temper. For Albert's part, he was a steady character – loyal to his wife and skilled at not rising to her provocations. This serious young German had a world-class political mind, and although Albert was disliked in some quarters simply for being a foreigner and for not enjoying sport or taking part in small talk, he soon impressed the likes of Lord Melbourne with his intellectual abilities, which would – once she let him use them – prove a boon for his young wife.

> *'I walked out with my precious Angel, all alone – so delightful, on the Terrace and new Walk, arm in arm! Eos our only companion. We talked a great deal together.'*
>
> ~VICTORIA'S JOURNAL, 11 FEBRUARY 1840

But the bond between Victoria and Albert wasn't only social and sexual; they had one other thing in common. Both were the products of broken homes. In addition, rumours persistently circulated that Albert was illegitimate. Albert's mother, Princess Louise of Saxe-Gotha-Altenburg, separated from her husband when Albert was only five years of age. She was exiled from the Saxe-Coburg court at Rosenau, and when she went she handed both her sons into their father's care. Albert had been the Princess's marked favourite, leading some historians to conclude that he was, indeed, a love child.

LEOPOLD:
I had just lost my beloved Charlotte and your father had left her all alone here with your brother, and … well … we comforted one another.

ALBERT:
At least Ernst knows who his father is.

IF HE WAS, there were two candidates for Louise's attention at the relevant time. One was the Baron von Mayern, the court chamberlain. Mayern was musical (like Albert) and sophisticated, but he was much older than the Princess and essentially a member of her household staff. The second candidate visited the Princess's home at the time when Albert would have been conceived – Prince Leopold of Saxe-Coburg and Gotha (who was both Victoria and Albert's uncle) spent several weeks at Rosenau over the winter after his wife, Princess Charlotte, died in childbirth. Louise wrote of his visit and of his being a widower, 'He still feels, with fervour, what it means to be happy and to be loved,' she said. She also asked a friend to tell her if she considered her husband or Prince Leopold to be the more handsome, saying, 'I love them both, only in different ways.'

There are no records to show whether or not Victoria was aware of the question hanging over Albert's legitimacy, but gossip at court was certainly always rife. The lives of all courtiers depended on the monarch and any such questions were the subject of excited interest. This threat of illegitimacy sheds light on Victoria and Albert's marital devotion and their horror of infidelity – an unusual attitude at the time in their circle. They took each other seriously and together faced the job in hand. Victoria was in frequent contact with Uncle Leopold – in fact, he helped arrange her marriage to Albert – so if she was aware of the rumours, she didn't hold them against him. She was also kind about Albert's mother, naming her fourth daughter Louise after her. Whether she did this because she adored her husband or because she simply didn't know the rumours about the Princess's behaviour, we just don't know.

TOM HUGHES
PLAYS
PRINCE ALBERT

'Victoria and Albert were young, passionate, idealistic; they both had the verve of youth and that was slightly scary for the Establishment that went before. Like any youth movement, it ruffled feathers. Coming into this position at such a young age would have brought challenges – Victoria would have been relatively isolated as a young woman and added to that Albert was in a foreign land. As a unit, it forces them to have this relentless drive to survive.'

ALBERT

'He has a passion, a verve . . . I'm enjoying delving into them.'

···· TOM HUGHES (PRINCE ALBERT) ····

LIKE VICTORIA, ALBERT'S childhood was not an entirely happy one. His parents' marriage was no love match and his father was a serial philanderer. Albert was more serious than his father or his brother, Ernst, did not indulge in heavy drinking (he took water with his meals) and showed no interest in any woman other than his wife. While Victoria was a night owl who loved to stay up dancing, Albert found much about court life tiresome, admitting, 'The late hours are what I find most difficult to bear.'

As the Queen's Consort, Albert was initially unpopular with the public and was disliked for being a foreigner. There was also opposition to Albert from within the Establishment, as his forward-thinking ideas were seen as a challenge. He was a competent political theoretician who pioneered the idea of a responsible and effective constitutional monarchy.

Albert also backed scientific and technological development, overhauled the management of the royal palaces and estates and influenced the contemporary English music and art scenes. However, in aristocratic circles these things mattered less than fitting in. Apart from a select few activities, such as stag hunting, he found most traditional upper-class pursuits boring, including riding, which Victoria loved. She convinced him to allow her to teach him to ride in the English fashion, and in 1843 when he rode with the Belvoir Hunt he acquitted himself well and was surprised at how much more accepted he was afterwards by the English upper classes.

Within a few years of his marriage, and after a deal of great political manoeuvring, Albert gradually won the Queen's trust. He had access to all royal papers, drafted the Queen's correspondence and attended ministerial meetings with her. A powerful figure in his own right, he was a formidable hard worker and a dedicated family man.

Albert will you marry me?

A S A CHILD, when Victoria first realised her proximity to the throne, she famously announced her intention 'to be good'. Her bravery in the face of repeated apparent assassination attempts inspired public confidence. In this vein, Victoria made it her business to put her royal weight behind several good causes, organising the Plantagenet Ball in support of the Spitalfields silk weavers (see pages 224–5), for example, and donating £2,000 towards Irish Famine Relief. Although her efforts weren't always successful, the fact that the Queen kept supporting causes she believed in meant that the public came to respect her engagement with what was going on in the country. Educated for the role from a young age, Victoria had a lively, enquiring mind and was well versed in history, religion and the arts, as well as popular novels – all of which may have strengthened her ability to understand and engage with the social issues of her day. Given Albert's fascination with science and innovation, the couple's education and interests complemented each other, and undoubtedly they made use of them, working much harder than the previous generations of royals to rule the country to the best of their abilities.

VICTORIA:
There were many people in my country who did not think that I could be Queen, but I never doubted it.

QUEEN VICTORIA'S LIBRARY

WHILE ALBERT HAD a full scientific education, the curriculum for Victoria when she was growing up was classical and arts-based, with a focus on languages. As a child under the Kensington System, Victoria had a reading list of 150 works. In a record dated 1826, the books include twenty religious texts, twenty-seven French books, thirteen volumes of classical Latin and grammar, the poetry of Dryden, Pope, Cowper, Shakespeare and Goldsmith, treatises in business and astronomy, Blackstone's classic *Commentaries on the Laws of England* and compendiums on geography, natural history and moral teachings.

When she became Queen, Victoria also became Head of the Church of England, and so, in preparation, by the age of nine she had learned the catechism of the Church of England by heart. By sixteen she had read Dryden's translation of *The Aeneid*, Pope's *Iliad*, Voltaire's *History of Charles XII* in the original French, and was studying Clarendon's *History of the Rebellion*, Goldsmith's histories of England, Greece and Rome and Magnall's *Historical and Miscellaneous Questions*.

Throughout her life, Victoria loved to read. As well as the classical books in her library, she enjoyed poetry and contemporary novels, especially those about the lives of ordinary people. Among her favourite authors was Dinah Craik, whose novel, *John Halifax, Gentleman,* was a particular favourite. Victoria recommended Mrs Craik to her daughter, Princess Victoria: 'Have you ever read two pretty, simple but very pleasantly written novels called *A Noble Life* by the authoress of *J. Halifax* and *Janet's Home*? They have both been read to me of an evening and I like them so much. Not sensation(al) novels but pretty, simple stories, full of truth and good feeling.'

Mrs Oliphant was another of the Queen's favourite authors, and with her love of all things Scottish, she greatly enjoyed her 1850 novel *Merkland*, which she described as 'an old but excellent Scotch novel'. In 1868 the Queen met Mrs Oliphant, whom she said was 'very pleasant and clever looking'. She also read Sir Walter Scott's novels and took at least one with her when she visited Scotland in 1842, later using his novels as inspiration when she and Albert set up Balmoral, their retreat in the north of Scotland. Victoria particularly enjoyed the poetry of Alfred, Lord Tennyson, who was Poet Laureate for over forty years during her reign.

Marie Corelli – a writer of popular novels – also appealed to the Queen. In conversation on one occasion, a courtier who disliked Corelli's work was mortified when the Queen came to the novelist's defence. Victoria was also a fan of Wilkie Collins, Charles Dickens and George Eliot, regardless of the latter's scandalous cohabitation with a married man.

....

Right: The Moonstone by Wilkie Collins, one of the Queen's favourite authors.
Below: One of the titles on Victoria's childhood study list, *Commentaries on the Laws of England*.

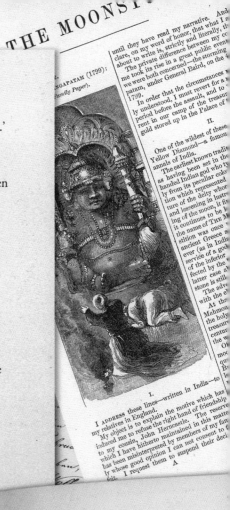

October 1839

'While I shall be untiring in my efforts and labours for the country to which I shall in future belong, and where I am called to so high a position, I shall never cease ein treuer Deutscher, Coburger, Gothaner zu sein.'

LETTER FROM ALBERT TO HIS STEP-GRANDMOTHER, PRINCESS KAROLINE AMALIE OF HESSE-KASSEL, UPON HIS ENGAGEMENT TO VICTORIA, ON 15 OCTOBER 1839

ON ALBERT'S PART, sound financial management of royal affairs stood his reputation in good stead when he had previously been portrayed as a German interloper who only wanted to get his hands on British power and money. 'I shall never cease to be a true German,' he said to Lord Aberdeen, and British cartoonists and satirists never let him forget it! Victoria's clear insistence that she was the Queen and her refusal to be entirely subsumed into the more traditional roles of wife and mother meant that she and Albert, despite ongoing criticism, quickly became viewed as a very modern couple. They were in love, they worked hard and tried their best, and as a result they were increasingly taken seriously by their subjects. During the early part of Victoria's reign, the advent of the pioneering medium of photography meant that day-to-day royal life in the palace was more accessible to Victoria's subjects than it had ever been before, and this contributed to the public goodwill that the couple earned over time.

TIMELINE OF NATIONAL EVENTS 1841–46

1841
- Robert Peel becomes prime minister
- New Zealand becomes an independent colony of Britain
- Victoria gives birth, aged twenty-two, to Albert, Prince of Wales
- Thomas Cook opens his travel agency
- The first issue of *Punch* hits the newsstands

1842
- Chartist strikes
- The end of the Opium War: Hong Kong ceded to Britain
- British defeat at Kabul and retreat during the First Afghan War
- The first peacetime income tax is brought in
- The term 'dinosaur' is coined by Richard Owen

1843
- William Wordsworth becomes Poet Laureate
- Britain annexes the southeastern African colony of Natal
- Victoria gives birth, aged twenty-four, to Princess Alice
- The *News of the World* and *The Economist* are first published
- Nelson's statue is erected in Trafalgar Square

1844
- Victoria gives birth, aged twenty-five, to Prince Alfred
- The YMCA is founded in London
- Ninety-five are killed in the Haswell Colliery explosion
- Victoria opens the Royal Exchange in London

1845
- The Irish Potato Famine begins
- 'Railway mania' takes hold as investment booms in railroad expansion
- Peel resigns as prime minister and is reinstated
- The last fatal duel in England is fought
- The First Anglo-Sikh War begins
- Building starts on Osborne House

1846
- Victoria gives birth, aged twenty-seven, to Princess Helena
- The railway line from London to York is begun
- The planet Neptune is first observed
- The first operation under anaesthetic takes place
- Peel resigns as prime minister in favour of Lord John Russell
- Waverley Station opens in Edinburgh
- Albert Dock opens in Liverpool

WHILE THE VICTORIAN era was a time of horrifying poverty for many, over the course of Victoria's reign there was also an increase in employment and human rights across the board, including for women and children. As its empire expanded, Britain became wealthier and social mobility increased. Thanks to the Industrial Revolution and to new markets opening up overseas, land was no longer the only source of wealth and the middle classes swelled. Literacy rates steadily rose – despite the fact that the Queen herself resisted compulsory education for the working classes. Cheap rail travel, huge improvements in housing for the majority and impressive events that focused the public's attention on the benefits of being British meant that many of Victoria's subjects enjoyed better lives than their forebears. They identified with their country and, in turn, identified their country with their queen.

Which is why, even though the direct political control that could be exercised by the royals dwindled throughout Victoria's reign, the public perception of royalty was revolutionised – without a revolution actually taking place. While the passionate love affair and family values Victoria and Albert demonstrated were genuine, it could be argued that it also saved the British monarchy from the fate of the many European royal houses that fell in the late 1840s. With grit and determination, together Victoria and Albert stood up for what they believed in and presented a shining example of a happy family life.

SIR ROBERT PEEL:
You don't need a crown, Sir, to do great things for this country.

COSTUME

'There are some very famous paintings of Albert, one of which is him in his wedding outfit, which is a red army uniform, a version of which still exists in Kensington Palace … After his death, Victoria had it embroidered with "my beloved Albert" and doves and hearts. There is also a famous Winterhalter painting of him in this beautiful dark blue long coat, and I had a version of that made for actor Tom Hughes and he looked spectacular in it.'

ROSALIND EBBUTT, COSTUME DESIGNER

Series two of *Victoria* runs from 1841 to 1846, and Rosalind Ebbutt, the series costume designer, has meticulously researched all costumes of the period, from children's dress to Victoria's state ballgowns, military uniforms (English, French and German all feature in the series) and servants' attire. Victoria also has several children during this period, so the team has a set of prosthetic bumps to cover all stages of pregnancy.

On the set in Yorkshire, the costume department is housed in a brick warehouse that covers around 3,500 square feet. There is a laundry and a sewing room in the building, which is frequently filled to capacity with costumes, looked after by a permanent staff of eight, which can swell to twelve for busy sequences. While starring actors dress in their own trucks, crowd scenes are fitted in the costume store, so on some days there might be large numbers of people passing through this brick building. The costume rails are crammed with labelled hangers, with 'French soldier' or 'Victoria – nursery scene' written in stickers on the stem, while numerous boxes contain piles of trimmed bonnets or military helmets.

Meticulous historical detail is important with every costume, so even the kitchen maids wear corsets and two petticoats under their dresses. Jenna Coleman, who plays Victoria, has several corsets made to measure for different purposes – including a riding corset that stops high enough on her ribcage to allow her to ride sidesaddle on location. For her designs, Rosalind Ebbutt consults paintings and prints from the era as well as surviving dresses, uniforms and accessories from the period. At a nearby museum she discovered a Victorian lady's maternity dress that she was excited to replicate. While some outfits are made to measure, costumes are also hired from different specialist sources and will then be fitted to individual actors. Turnarounds can be very quick, and it's not unheard of for a dress to be commissioned, designed, tailored, fitted and completed within a week.

On set, Buckingham Palace has been newly kitted out with its own costume department of sorts – a bonnet room, a dresser's room and a boot room, all based on the real 'behind-the-scenes' areas of Victoria's life. Hundreds of people were employed at the palace to make clothes, polish boots, trim accessories and keep the royal family's linen in good order. An embroidered cape might take weeks of painstaking expert work to complete by hand.

CHAPTER 2

THE NEVER-ENDING LOVE AFFAIR

'Victoria was very lucky. In Albert she found someone who loved her for herself . . . he found her physically attractive.'

···· DAISY GOODWIN, SCREENWRITER OF *VICTORIA* ····

WHEN VICTORIA PROPOSED to Albert in October 1839, he gave the young Queen Britain's first engagement ring – the start of a succession of love tokens over the years and an act that has had a lasting impact on expectations of romance for every couple. She was smitten. When Victoria announced to her court her intention to marry Albert, she admitted that she was nervous – terrified, even. She wore a gold bracelet inlaid with a miniature portrait of her future husband to give her strength and later said it made her feel that he was with her when she wore it. Victoria was the first royal bride to wear a white wedding dress, thereby founding another tradition as well as a multi-million-pound industry. Victoria and Albert were famously devoted to each other. Neither of them had seen a genuinely happy domestic situation in practice – Victoria had been brought up under the stringent Kensington System, while Albert had grown up at Rosenau with an absent mother and neglectful father. While there is less written evidence of Albert's love of his wife, he spent huge amounts of time with her and was not shy of making a romantic gesture. When Victoria gave him a flower as they were dancing at a ball during their courtship, he found he had nowhere to put it, so he took a knife, cut a slit in his uniform over his heart and slipped the bloom in there.

VICTORIA DID NOT 'lie back and think of England'. The Queen's diary after her wedding reveals a strong interest in the physical side of their relationship. She noted eagerly on the day before their marriage that this would be 'the last time I slept alone'. It's interesting that even on such an important and private day, Victoria still made time to write in her journal, where she records that a passionate relationship ensued between herself and her husband, and confided that the wedding night was 'bliss beyond belief'. It's perplexing that Victoria's reign is commonly thought of as prudish when the Queen herself took such pleasure in sex.

During the first series of *Victoria* we saw the newly married Queen jumping up and down in the middle of the night to try and avoid pregnancy. The truth is there was no avoiding the duties of childbearing for an aristocratic British woman of her time. Contraceptives were available throughout Victoria's reign in the form of makeshift condoms, but no respectable woman would use them and most weren't even aware of the possibility. Also, Victorians thought women, like dogs, were most fertile during menstruation – the exact opposite of the truth. Bearing children within marriage was seen as a woman's duty, and no one had more of a duty in that regard than the Queen herself. Ultimately, Victoria succumbed to the pleasures of the marital bed and enjoyed herself, despite the fact that quite early on in her marriage she realised she hated childbirth and was not interested in babies. The 'fun' element was the most important thing to her.

BARONESS LEHZEN:
Is it possible, Majesty, that you are to be blessed again?

VICTORIA:
Don't be absurd, Lehzen. I've just had a baby.

'His beauty, his sweetness and gentleness — really how can I ever be thankful enough to have such a Husband!'

VICTORIA'S JOURNAL THE DAY AFTER HER WEDDING NIGHT, 11 FEBRUARY 1840

SEX FOR SALE

THE VICTORIAN ERA has a reputation for being strait-laced, a time when formal middle-class life conformed to respectability in all things, but scratch the surface and there was a racy undertone – almost a secret world. In Georgian times, London had been awash with private clubs that could accommodate a variety of sexual interests. By Victoria's reign these clubs were on the wane, but all the major cities had red-light districts where it was easy to find sex for sale. Out-of-towners could consult guidebooks like Roger Funnyman's *The Swell's Night Guide through the Metropolis* to find what they were looking for. Such volumes contained intimate details about what was on offer in different establishments. Some common practices were thought extraordinarily racy at the time – oral sex, for example, was considered one of the filthiest activities and was sometimes referred to as a 'foreign practice'.

The spectre of the prostitute haunted middle-class homes, not only before marriage but also during it, partly because prostitutes were so difficult to spot. While there were a few places in London where women stood on the street to sell themselves, far more prevalent was a group of respectable-looking women, living together and 'hiring out'. This was called 'sly prostitution' and there are no accurate records of how many women were engaged in the practice. Doctors of the day were extremely worried by the 'problem' prostitution presented, in particular the rise of venereal disease among the male population, who often then transmitted diseases to their wives. To combat the situation, the Contagious Diseases Act of 1860 allowed the forced medical examination of any woman who was suspected of being a sex worker. If infected, the woman could be placed in a specialist 'lock hospital' until she was cured.

A reform movement led by campaigner Josephine Butler vigorously called for a repeal of the Act, arguing that it was male clients who were responsible for the problem – why not lock them up?

Society, however, did not agree and many charities were instituted to 'reform' prostitutes. For example, Charles Dickens collaborated with the heiress and philanthropist Angela Burdett-Coutts to set up a 'Magdalen House' to train prostitutes in other trades to prepare them for a new life in Australia. Despite these efforts, prostitution continued to flourish. Single mothers were looked down upon and social censure was so grave that most handed over their babies to the Foundling Hospital in London or, horrifyingly, killed their newborn children in desperation. For many, prostitution was a way out of poverty and one of the few ways they could make enough money to build a better life.

For men looking for less direct titillation than prostitutes provided, burlesque shows were a speciality. First seen in New York in the very early years of Victoria's reign, burlesque soon made it to Britain when London's Gaiety Theatre and the Royal Strand Theatre ran pastiche parodies of popular songs, operas and other music performed by saucy, scantily-clad young ladies. The up-and-coming medium of photography was also making pornography easier to distribute, and today there are huge archives of this material – a testament to its popularity.

....

Right: A publication detailing the naughty goings-on and salacious gossip of racy Victorian London.

THE DAYS' DOINGS.

An Illustrated Journal of Romantic Events, Reports, Sporting & Theatrical News at Home & Abroad.

PUBLISHED AT No. 300, STRAND, LONDON, W.C.—SATURDAY, JUNE 24, 1871.

[PRICE THREEPENCE.
Registered at the G.P.O. as a Newspaper.

VOL. II.—No. 48.]
All Rights Reserved.

AWKWARD CONTRE-TEMPS IN REGENT STREET DURING THE HEIGHT OF THE SEASON.
"That Girl seems to know you, George!"

THE YOUNG QUEEN could be jealous, and her suspicions were aroused if Albert so much as talked to another woman. She suspected several young ladies at court of flirting with her husband, including the stately Elizabeth, Marchioness of Douro, and Maids of Honour Harriet Pitt and Mary Spring Rice, the latter of whom liked to chat to Prince Albert to practise her German. Olivia, the pretty daughter of the 2nd Marquess of Headfort, was packed off home when Victoria noticed the way that the young Irishwoman spoke to Albert. Later, Olivia became Lady Fitzpatrick and it was said of her that 'she would start a flirtation with St Paul under the eyes of the Deity'. Albert, however, never responded to such interest. The idea of a relationship outside of marriage was unthinkable – his childhood made him terrified of infidelity.

The young couple treasured their privacy. In a palace with almost a thousand staff, it's easy to see why – royal lives were conducted in public and Victoria had been heavily supervised throughout her childhood. She had enjoyed almost no personal space, and Albert was now protective of that space, objecting to intrusions into the royal bedchamber by Baroness Lehzen and other staff. Clearly the royal couple's physical relationship was a priority for them both.

> '... I expect [Albert] back at about eleven tonight. He went at half past eleven this morning. It is the first time that we have ever been separated for so long since our marriage, and I am quite melancholy about it.'
>
> ~LETTER FROM VICTORIA TO LEOPOLD, THE KING OF THE BELGIANS, 8 AUGUST 1841

This passion was sparked in other areas of their domestic life, too, when the couple fought. Arguments might be about domestic arrangements – certainly when Albert objected to Baroness Lehzen's influence in the nursery, he and Victoria had a protracted fight about it (see pages 118–19) – but in fact they argued over a wide range of

ALBERT:
Where are
you going?

VICTORIA:
To the nursery,
Albert. Isn't that
where you think
I belong?

subjects and situations. Victoria felt left out of Albert's scientific interests. While she had benefited from a wide-ranging classical education she could not always join him in mathematical or scientific debate, and she found this frustrating. More than anything, however, in these early years they argued about Albert's role.

'The sky will not always be blue and unclouded. But life has its thorns …'
~LETTER FROM ALBERT TO HIS STEPMOTHER AND COUSIN,
DUCHESS MARIE OF WÜRTTENBERG, 5 NOVEMBER 1839

Albert had been slighted by Parliament from the beginning of the marriage, when the House of Commons chose to accord him an allowance of £30,000 as opposed to the usual amount for a royal spouse of £50,000. Parliament also overruled Victoria's wish that Albert be accorded the title of King as opposed to Prince Consort. Albert accepted these constrictions and later, once he had proved himself, Parliament upped his allowance. In an atmosphere where his skills were not immediately valued he faced an uphill battle in finding something worthwhile to do. He wanted to help Victoria rule (though Britain was by this time a constitutional monarchy and even the Queen had limited power), but Victoria was highly sensitive to anyone (Albert included) encroaching on her duties. She had refused to delete the promise 'to obey' her husband from her wedding vows, wanting to conform to what was a normal marriage for the day. In practice though, she found herself torn between enjoying domestic bliss and feeling that her authority was being undermined by pregnancy after pregnancy. While the Queen was engaged in the business of childbirth and its aftermath, Albert took over her duties. Victoria resented this not only because she was the Queen, but also because she wanted him to be at her bedside, spending time with her. While they never fought in full public view, their arguments were an open secret at the palace and servants, staff and courtiers could not help but witness their heated exchanges.

VICTORIA:
It may be your regiment, Albert, but it is my army.

RUFUS SEWELL

PLAYS
LORD MELBOURNE

'I think one of the reasons Melbourne and Victoria immediately got on so well was that I don't think she'd met anyone before that would take her at her word. No one had listened to her and given her credence in that way. Melbourne was very successful but he was also a very kind man and well liked.'

LORD MELBOURNE

'He was everything to her for a while.'

···• RUFUS SEWELL (MELBOURNE) •···

WHEN VICTORIA'S BELOVED Lord M resigned as prime minister in 1841 it didn't by any means mark the end of their relationship. Indeed, correspondence between them continued on a daily basis, which many considered inappropriate. For the Queen, however, the friendship was vital. She was devastated when Melbourne resigned and burst into tears on the terrace at Windsor Castle the evening he left. Melbourne tried to be cheerful. The four years he'd had with Victoria were, he declared, the happiest and proudest of his life. But Victoria never really let her favourite prime minister go, and tongues continued to wag in the palace and beyond.

'My poor good Ld Melbourne, … was looking well in health, but alas! has such a sadly vacant look in his eyes, which it grieves me so to see.'

~VICTORIA'S JOURNAL, 1 DECEMBER 1843

Inevitably perhaps, Victoria's reliance on Melbourne's advice resulted in gossip. She was publicly referred to as 'Mrs Melbourne' on more than one occasion – crowds shouted the name at her as she rode past in her coach, and when she arrived at Ascot with Melbourne in tow it was hurled from the stands. Magazines circulated showing a cartoon of Melbourne as landlord of the 'Windsor Arms' and Victoria peering down from an upstairs bedroom. Nonetheless, the Queen continued to seek political advice from her beloved Lord M as well as sharing family news and gossip with him. Over time, their letters contained less and less politics.

In the years after he left office, Melbourne's health declined. He was ageing and overweight, and though he continued to attend balls at the palace, the correspondence between him and Victoria gradually became more infrequent and had all but ceased by 1845. He died of a stroke at Brocket Hall in 1848 and, as his children had predeceased him, his title passed to his brother, Frederick.

ALBERT:
How can you
believe that writing
to Melbourne is
anything but foolish?
The Whigs are out of
office, to write to him
is unconstitutional.

ICTORIA AND ALBERT both cultivated their own camps. Victoria continued to write to Lord Melbourne for political advice, which Lord M handled with delicacy, while Albert was closer to the new Tory prime minister, Sir Robert Peel, which helped Peel in some of his reforms. Ever a perfectionist, when he undertook state business on behalf of his wife Albert agonised over each situation, trying to find the perfect solution. He laboured over complex filing systems for the royal papers, as well as editing and transcribing letters obsessively – all of which points to his determination to do well. Early in their marriage, issues like the British defeat in Afghanistan and the British victory in China provided plenty of fodder for debate between the couple. They also had fun and joked about making 'Pussy', their eldest daughter, Vicky, Princess of Hong Kong when it was ceded to Great Britain in 1842.

'I thank God you have such an excellent husband, so well calculated to make you happy and to assist you in your arduous duties by his advice, as well as his help in sharing your troubles. I pray that your domestic happiness may last …'

~LETTER FROM VICTORIA'S AUNT, QUEEN ADELAIDE,
TO VICTORIA, VALENTINE'S DAY, 1843

However, the arguments were ongoing, and Victoria – a passionate woman in all things – was vocal in her anger, slamming doors and shouting. Albert was a more repressed personality and when his wife lost her temper he would usually retreat. There was a medical fear voiced at the time that if Victoria became too distressed she might succumb to the madness of George III (her grandfather). If the Queen lost her mind, the very institution of the monarchy would be threatened. While this concern was not valid in the light of modern medical understanding, there is no question that Albert had been briefed about it and that it was part of his decision to stand down when arguments with his wife became heated.

USUALLY THE QUEEN would eventually relent. She adored her husband, after all, and ultimately valued his input and was desperate for him to be embraced by the public. She looked forward to their daily walk in the grounds of the palace, where they could be alone. Over time, she allowed him not only to work with her on the Parliamentary boxes delivered to the palace, but also to attend ministerial meetings. At Osborne House, Albert had a double door built into the room where ministerial meetings were held so that the couple could arrive simultaneously – which was done with the Queen's consent. Initially when Victoria expressed her views, she did so in the singular 'I', but quickly she moved to what we now know as 'the royal we', by which she meant herself and Albert. Albert was 'king' at home in the royal palace, if not in the wider country.

MELBOURNE:
I did not want you to be overshadowed. Yes, the Prince is your husband, but you are The Queen.

'I wish you could see us here and see in us a couple united in love and unanimity. Now Victoria is also ready to give up something for my sake, I everything for her sake … Do not think I lead a submissive life. On the contrary, here, where the lawful position of the man is so, I have formed a prize life for myself.'

UNDATED LETTER FROM ALBERT TO HIS BROTHER, ERNST, BEFORE THE BIRTH OF PRINCESS VICTORIA

VICTORIA:
Actually, Uncle Leopold, what my country needs right now is a queen, not a brood mare.

THIS DIDN'T MAKE the arguments any easier. Albert was of a serious bent and in dealing with Victoria's temper he often sounded like a schoolteacher. In one letter, he praised her 'unbroken success of self-control' when she had a period of not losing her temper. Often he would simply walk away and then afterwards write to Victoria, begging her to talk rationally and see his point of view. On one occasion he locked his door and wouldn't let Victoria in until she asked him 'as his wife', not 'as the Queen'. For her part, Victoria wrote long letters of apology for her bad behaviour and begged Albert's forgiveness. They always made up in the end.

It should be said that the situation in which the royal couple found themselves was unique in its day. For the women under Victoria's rule, their husband's word was law, quite literally. On reaching adulthood, women passed from the care of a father into the care of a husband, and it was often only in widowhood that they gained any measure of self-determination. Even working women had no right to the money they earned. Until the Married Women's Property Act of 1870, everything a married woman earned legally belonged to her husband. It wasn't until the Act of 1882 that she could retain her own property once she was married. Victoria's royal position accorded her the tremendous privilege of control over her professional life and her own purse strings. It's little wonder she stood up for that but also, given the social norms of the day, understandable that she ultimately often deferred to Albert.

TIMELINE OF
WOMEN'S HISTORY
IN THE 1800S

DURING THE VICTORIAN period, the roles of men and women became more sharply defined than at any other time in history. In earlier centuries it had been usual for ordinary middle-class women to work alongside their husbands and brothers in the family business, but as the nineteenth century progressed men increasingly commuted to their place of work – the factory, shop or office – and their wives, daughters and sisters were left at home. By contrast, the stories of working-class women highlight the discrepancy between the country's wealth and its appalling social conditions. Women were beginning to earn wages in mills and factories for the first time and economic independence meant political momentum was gained for women's rights.

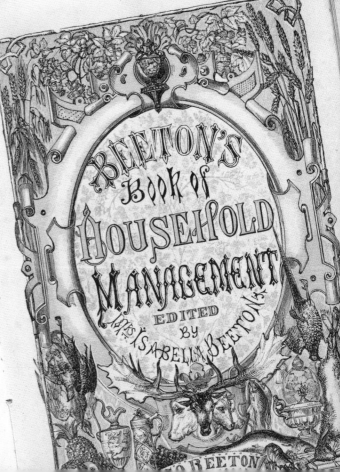

....
Right: Mrs Beeton's *Book of Household Management*, first published in 1861. Above: Prints by female writer and illustrator Beatrix Potter, which went on sale in 1893.

1837 ◈ Queen Victoria comes to the throne

1840 ◈ Elizabeth Fry opens a training school for nurses
1840 ◈ Romantic ballet becomes fashionable. Victoria adores Marie Taglioni
1842 ◈ Ada Lovelace writes the first computer program
1844 ◈ The Factory Act cuts women's hours to no more than twelve per day
1847 ◈ The Brontë sisters are first published
1848 ◈ Harriet Martineau publishes her book *Household Education*, about the rights of women

1853 ◈ Women gain legal protection from domestic violence
1853 ◈ Queen Victoria uses chloroform for pain relief during the birth of Leopold
1853 ◈ Elizabeth Gaskell publishes *Cranford*
1854 ◈ Isabella Bird writes books about her solo trips all over the world
1855 ◈ Mary Seacole sets up field hospitals in the Crimean War
1857 ◈ The Matrimonial Causes Act grants women limited access to divorce

1861 ◈ Mrs Beeton's *Book of Household Management* is first published
1865 ◈ Marie Bancroft manages the Prince of Wales's Theatre
1866 ◈ John Stuart Mill campaigns with the Women's Suffrage Committee to get women the vote
1869 ◈ Edinburgh University admits the first women to medical school
1869 ◈ Single women ratepayers are allowed to vote in local elections

1870 ◈ The Married Women's Property Act decrees that women can keep the money they earn after marriage
1870 ◈ The first condom factory producing rubber condoms opens in Dalston
1874 ◈ Sophia Jex-Blake and Elizabeth Garrett Anderson found the Women's School for Medicine
1878 ◈ The Matrimonial Causes Act decrees that men must financially support their wives and children
1879 ◈ Oxford names one of its first women's colleges Somerville College after scientist Mary Somerville

1881 ◈ The Rational Dress Society publishes its gazette arguing for comfortable clothes for women
1882 ◈ The Married Women's Property Act allows women to keep their money and property after marriage
1889 ◈ *Hints to Lady Travellers* by Lillias Campbell Davidson is published

1890 ◈ Alice Bodington publishes her book on Darwin
1893 ◈ Prints of Benjamin Bunny by Beatrix Potter first go on sale
1895 ◈ Lilian Lindsay qualifies as the first female dentist

DUCHESS OF KENT:
I thought that
motherhood would
make her less difficult,
but it has only made
her worse. She is
rude to everyone,
including Albert.

ESPITE THEIR STORMY relationship, Victoria and Albert were clearly extremely happy, and while arguments blew up with regularity, they were usually settled quickly. The royal couple were generous with each other and often gave each other gifts – sometimes as part of the making-up process, sometimes to mark an occasion or simply because they wanted to express their love. These gifts form a kind of journal of their life together. Typically, they commissioned items, making them extremely personal. For example, Victoria ordered a silver model of Albert's greyhound, Eos, in 1840, and also commissioned the favoured royal painter Edwin Landseer to paint Eos and gave the resulting portrait to Albert for Christmas the following year. In 1843 she posed for a 'boudoir' painting by fashionable artist Franz Xaver Winterhalter, choosing a not-very-royal and rather sexy pose, with her hair trailing over her shoulder. She gave this painting to Albert as a present on his twenty-fourth birthday and he kept it in his private rooms at Windsor Castle. After Albert's death Victoria wrote that it was 'my darling Albert's favourite picture'. The portrait was considered so racy that it was never put on public display during the Queen's lifetime. In it Victoria is wearing a locket that contained a lock of Albert's hair.

Over the years, despite Victoria's reputation for being prudish, the couple collected several extraordinarily erotic paintings, including a number of nudes by William Edward Frost, many of which were hung in the public rooms of their various homes. Victoria also ordered a statue of Lady Godiva by French sculptor Pierre-Emile Jeannest, whose work Albert admired, and gave it to her husband as a birthday gift in 1857. When the Queen commissioned Scottish artist William Dyce to paint a fresco entitled *Neptune Resigning to Britannia the Empire of the Sea* – a scene of writhing male and female nudes – Dyce said that Prince Albert was shocked. More privately, though, in Albert's bathroom at Osborne House there is an astonishing mural of Hercules in bondage to Queen Omphale.

MANY OF THE items in the book and the series are still in the Royal Collection. The Collection is a unique record of the personal tastes of kings and queens over the past 500 years and includes the majority of the contents of some thirteen royal residences and former residences across the UK, most of which are regularly open to the public. These include Windsor Castle, Buckingham Palace, Kensington Palace, Osborne House and the Royal Pavilion, Brighton.

......

Top left: Albert's greyhound Eos by Edwin Landseer.
Above right: A miniature of Albert produced In 1840.
Left: Painted by Franz Xaver Winterhalter, Albert hung this 24th birthday present from Victoria in his private rooms.

THE MATTER OF ERNST

*'Even in infancy a marked difference was observable ...
their separate paths were definitely marked out, yet ... seems to have
afforded a closer bond of union between them. Mr Florschutz,
Albert and Ernst's tutor on his charges as children.'*

MEMORANDUM, 23 NOVEMBER 1823

THE SECOND SERIES does not cover Albert's brother's marriage, which took place on 3 May 1842 when he married Princess Alexandrine of Baden. Ernst was a tricky figure for those closest to him. Like his father, and in contrast to Albert, he had been a notorious womaniser throughout his teens and twenties and had fully sampled the delights of both Paris and Berlin, at his father's insistence. When he visited London in 1839 one of Victoria's ladies-in-waiting observed that Ernst was 'very thin and hollow-cheeked and pale, and no likeness to his brother'.

In fact, he was suffering from a venereal disease. Albert was furious and warned his brother not to seek a wife until his condition was cured. However, syphilis, from which Ernst suffered, is a complex disease. In its early stages the patient suffers from rashes and sores but as it progresses the symptoms become more serious, with high temperature, changes in vision, hair loss, and ultimately it affects the heart and central nervous system and can lead to tumours. In the Victorian era it was incurable. Ernst tried – he underwent mercury steam baths, the treatment of the day – but to little effect. Albert raged that Ernst's continued promiscuity might render him unable to father children, but he did in fact have at least three illegitimate children and probably more. This was not unusual for aristocrats at the time. The Duke, Ernst and Albert's father, had also fathered illegitimate issue – at least four children are on record, by three different women.

RACY VICTORIANS BEHIND CLOSED DOORS

WHILE SUPERFICIALLY VICTORIAN society was relatively prudish, the lines between respectable women and those on the make were more blurred than many historians like to admit. Throughout Victoria's rule there was a rainbow of relationship arrangements in existence. Without the ease of divorce, many couples in 'second' relationships could never be entirely open about what was going on. Some women were set up in houses by their married lovers and referred to as 'kept', and the moral duty of a man to provide for his 'kept' lady was generally recognised along the lines of a 'common law marriage'. Another practice was that of keeping a 'common' woman, a scenario in which several men might contribute to a woman's upkeep and all demand sexual favours from her.

In the upper classes many couples had affairs that were pursued privately at house parties – once a wife had provided an heir and a spare, she was often considered free to take a lover if she so wished. In practice, this was not openly acknowledged, but if a group were staying for a few days in a large, aristocratic house, it might be expected that, once everyone had gone to bed, couples would creep along the corridors to have illicit sex. High- or low-class, people were pragmatic about such arrangements, and as long as they were discreet, couples could do whatever they liked. This even happened in royal residences, though Victoria was probably not aware of it. When Albert took over the management of the royal houses, however, he changed the sleeping arrangements, making midnight assignations more difficult to achieve.

It's worth noting that for most of Victoria's reign homosexuality was only illegal if it was practised 'in public'. You could get up to what you liked behind closed doors. Later in Victoria's reign the law changed and in 1885 homosexuality was made illegal, even in private. The writer Oscar Wilde was in one of the first waves of men to be imprisoned when his affair with Lord Alfred Douglas was publicised in 1895. Lord Alfred was sent abroad for several months by his family to remove him from the scandal, while Wilde was detained at Reading Gaol.

This shows how much attitudes varied over the course of Victoria's reign – the 1860s, for example, was a particularly laid-back decade. The 1890s were also famously liberal, and were nicknamed the 'Naughty Nineties' for good reason – unless you were gay. However, it's easy to forget in looking at the underbelly of Victorian life how hearty and accepting it could be. The female distaste evidenced by one woman's supposed advice to her newly married daughter to 'lie back and think of England' was not the norm, and many married women enjoyed fulfilling sex lives with their husbands – just as Victoria did.

....

Right: A Victorian prostitute raising a glass.

15 November 1839

'Even in my dreams I never imagined that I should find so much love on earth.'

LETTER FROM ALBERT TO VICTORIA DURING THEIR
ENGAGEMENT, 15 NOVEMBER 1839 (WRITTEN IN GERMAN)

ALBERT FAVOURED JEWELLERY when he chose gifts for Victoria. The day before their wedding in 1840 he gave her a sapphire and diamond brooch. Victoria said it was 'really quite beautiful' and wore it on her wedding dress alongside the gold and porcelain orange blossom sprig he had sent her on their engagement, with a piece of music he had written especially for her. Over the years, he continued to give Victoria pieces of jewellery to match the orange blossom set, the flower being considered an aphrodisiac and widely thought to be lucky. In 1845 Victoria received a second orange blossom brooch and a pair of matching earrings as a Christmas present. She wrote in her journal, 'My beloved one gave me such a lovely unexpected present ... with four little green enamel oranges meant to represent our children.' Later, more oranges were added as the family grew. Albert exercised his artistic talents and sometimes even designed pieces especially for his wife, including a pair of pear-shaped pearl drop earrings hanging from a diamond stud that he gave to her in 1847, and a brooch made out of a portrait of the Princess Royal as a baby inset into angel wings studded with gemstones. Princess Victoria later explained that 'Papa gave it to Mama . . . she always wore it on my birthday.'

Victoria certainly loved jewels, but she prized all gifts from her husband equally, regardless of their monetary value, and would dote upon items made from the milk teeth of the Princes and Princesses quite as much as those made from diamonds. More touching than any of the artefacts the royal couple left behind, however, are their letters to each other – tender, caring and, sometimes, even erotic.

PRINCE ALBERT'S TIARA

'My beloved one gave me such alovely unexpected present — a wreath, going rightaround the head, made to match the brooch and earrings he gave me at Christmas.'

VICTORIA'S JOURNAL, CHRISTMAS 1845

WHEN VICTORIA CAME to the throne she inherited the magnificent royal collections of jewels, which, during her sixty-four-year reign, expanded exponentially with gifts from the burgeoning empire, including the famous 186-carat uncut Koh-i-Noor diamond from India – now part of the Crown Jewels – which she received in 1849. Albert was fascinated by the Koh-i-Noor and, along with the Duke of Wellington, took an active interest in how the stone was to be cut to the best effect. He consulted with the leading gemologists and lapidologists of his day. The Queen also purchased jewellery in her own right and received presents from Albert, who enjoyed designing gifts for his wife, including the four tiaras or diadems he presented her with during the course of their marriage.

One of the most significant of these was an emerald, diamond and gold tiara that Albert commissioned in 1845 from goldsmith Joseph Kitching. The tiara cost £1,150 – over half a million pounds in today's money – and was designed by Albert in the Gothic Revival style. It features upright cabochon (meaning polished but not faceted) emeralds, probably sourced from Colombia. The cabochons are in the *vesica piscis* shape, which literally means 'the bladder of a fish', and are set on a base of scrolls with a triple layer of gemstones in the circlet, and one layer of baguette-cut emeralds with a layer of brilliant-cut diamonds on either side. It seems Albert simply gave his wife this gift without ceremony, rather than waiting for a special occasion – perhaps he was too excited to wait.

When Victoria posed for Franz Xaver Winterhalter's portrait of the royal family in 1846 she wore the tiara and also sported earrings and three brooches to match. Later, she was painted again wearing the tiara, accessorising it this time with other jewels. It's no surprise that it was one of her favourite pieces, not only because of its great value, but because Albert had had it made especially for her.

The emerald and diamond tiara remains in the private collection of one of Victoria's descendants and was loaned to the Historic Royal Palaces in 2017.

....

Opposite: Detail of a family portrait painted by Franz Xaver Winterhalter in 1846 depicting Victoria wearing the emerald and diamond tiara designed by Prince Albert.

THE LANGUAGE OF
FLOWERS

THE SYMBOLISM OF flowers was a highly popular way to send a 'secret' message in Victorian times, especially a romantic one. Reporting on the marriage of Queen Victoria and Prince Albert on 10 February 1840, *The Times* newspaper noted, 'Her Majesty wore no diamonds on her head, nothing but a simple wreath of orange blossom.' The Queen's modest floral adornment was an emblem of chastity and also widely believed to be an aphrodisiac. It spawned a fashion for orange blossom jewellery, like the brooch Albert had given Victoria before their wedding day, and over the years he added to his wife's collection. Victoria also had a Minton pen tray decorated with pansies, which were said to symbolise loving thoughts. She would have been well aware of this symbolism.

Victoria's favourite flower, however, is believed to be the violet – it's certainly the one mentioned most often in her diary. She had two baskets adorned with violets when she was a child, and often picked both primroses and violets in the gardens at Osborne House and elsewhere. Violets meant 'modesty' in the language of flowers, hence the phrase 'shrinking violet'. Primroses, on the other hand, meant 'I can't live without you!'

Victoria often wore real flowers in her hair, and wreath-making was a valued skill among her ladies.

The craze for secret messages in flower form started in 1825 when the botanist Henry Phillips wrote the first book in English about the meaning of different flowers. Quickly, Victorian lovers learned the code:

....

Above: Forget-me-not. Opposite: Sweet violet.

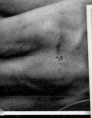

SWEET VIOLET.—*Viola oporata.*

FLOWER MEANINGS:

Begonia: *Beware*

White carnation: *Purity, True love, Innocence*

Pink carnation: *I will never forget you*

Red carnation: *Admiration*

Chrysanthemum and/or crocuses: *Cheerfulness*

Daffodil: *Unrequited love*

Fern: *Magic, Fascination*

Forget-me-not: *Memories*

Gardenia: *Secret love*

Geranium: *Folly*

Holly: *Domestic happiness*

Hyacinth: *Games and sport*

Iris: *Friendship, Hope*

Ivy: *Marriage, Fidelity*

Larkspur: *Fickleness*

Lily (Calla): *Beauty*

Magnolia: *Nobility*

Marigold: *Cruelty*

Myrtle: *Love*

Nasturtium: *Conquest*

Poppy: *Oblivion, Imagination*

Primrose: *I can't live without you*

Rose (tea rose): *I will remember*

Yellow rose: *Joy, Friendship*

Snapdragon: *Deception*

Zinnia (white): *Goodness*

CHAPTER 3
THE EXPECTANT QUEEN

'*It seems like a dream, having a child.*'

···· VICTORIA'S JOURNAL, 20 DECEMBER 1840 ····

PREGNANCY AND CHILDBIRTH were the greatest risks taken by women in Victoria's reign. In 1840, when Victoria had her first child in her bedroom at Buckingham Palace, five in every thousand births resulted in the death of the mother. Women quite literally took their lives in their hands when they entered the birthing chamber. Surviving one childbirth was no guarantee of surviving the next, and many women also suffered difficulties afterwards. Victoria was well aware of several mothers in her court circle who had post-partum health problems – in 1839, the year before Victoria and Albert married, she mentions four such aristocratic women in her diary. High rank was no protection against complications, and medical help for women undergoing pregnancy and labour was limited. There was no pain relief and very few procedures available to help if things went wrong.

The spectre of what had happened to 'poor' Princess Charlotte – daughter of George IV and wife of Prince Leopold – who had died at the age of twenty-one in 1817 after the delivery of a stillborn son still haunted the court. Though this had happened before Victoria herself was born, she knew of it and had discussed Charlotte's tragic death with Lord Melbourne. Until the birth of Victoria's first child, Princess Charlotte's lying-in was the last time a senior British royal had given birth. It's easy to see why the young Queen was apprehensive and why she referred to pregnancy in her diary as 'an unhappy condition'. Every time Victoria announced she was with child the whole court was forced to contemplate what would happen if the Queen did not survive.

VICTORIAN PREGNANCY AND CHILDBIRTH

IN VICTORIAN TIMES, both mother and child faced grave risks, especially if there were complications at or after the birth. The household guru of the day, Isabella Beeton, was a prime example of this – her first two children died in infancy and she herself perished, aged just twenty-eight, after giving birth to her fourth child. On average, a Victorian woman would have eight pregnancies in her lifetime, resulting in five living children. In 1842, when it became common practice for doctors to clean their hands before examining new mothers, childbirth mortality dropped from 18 per cent to only 6 per cent.

Medical knowledge of pregnancy and childbirth at the time was still dangerously lacking. There was, for example, no understanding that either alcohol or drugs were a danger to the foetus, or that wearing a corset might have medical implications for pregnant women. If they survived pregnancy, women were sometimes subjected to blood-letting on the birthing bed – a particularly damaging practice as many of them had ongoing nutritional deficiencies, as no prenatal vitamins were available. Indeed, Victorian nutritional advice for mothers-to-be was laughable – women were told that what they ate might affect their child's personality and so were counselled against 'sour and salty' foods, like pickles, in case this resulted in a baby with a bad disposition.

By the late 1840s the science of anaesthesia was beginning to revolutionise childbirth, offering women an escape from this so-called 'punishment'. Victoria had wanted to try chloroform since she had first heard of it at the time of her sixth confinement, but her obstetrician, Charles Locock, had counselled against it. With Albert's support, though, and the help of pioneering medical practitioner John Snow, the Queen availed herself of this new method at the birth of her eighth child in 1853. Incredibly, this was only possible by special permission from the Archbishop of Canterbury. Victoria inhaled the drug for fifty-three minutes from a handkerchief and was very happy with the results. She called it 'that blessed chloroform', said it was 'delightful beyond measure' and believed she recovered from the birth more quickly because of the pain relief. Her royal blessing ensured that many women then turned to chloroform to alleviate the pain of childbirth, and the Archbishop of Canterbury's own daughter used it when she went into labour.

The recovery time for Victorian ladies after giving birth was commonly four to six weeks. Victoria refused to breastfeed her children and considered it the 'ruin' of intellectual and refined young ladies. But, in fact, breastfeeding provides the mother with a measure of contraceptive protection, so had Victoria breastfed she might have substantially reduced her chances of getting so swiftly pregnant again.

DUKE OF SAXE-
COBURG:
Pity she is only
a girl, but
plenty of time,
eh, Albert?

DESPITE THIS, VICTORIA seems to have enjoyed her early pregnancies more than those that came later, and initially her excitement at the prospect of having a child leaps off the pages of her journal. 'How little I thought when I received him on the staircase that evening and beheld those eyes which seemed to go to my soul then, that I should not only be his wife but in the eighth month of my pregnancy on this same day, this year,' she wrote in August 1840, clearly unable to believe how quickly she had gone from being a single woman to a wife and expectant mother – both paragons of what every woman should be, according to the society of the day. Her health was good – she didn't complain in her diaries of morning sickness or other ailments associated with childbearing – she adored Albert and they were invested together in starting a family, so there was cause for optimism.

This does not mean that the Queen was not under pressure. Quite apart from the dangers associated with childbirth, Victoria was expected to produce a male heir to secure the line of succession. She admitted in her diary that she and Albert were 'sadly disappointed' when their first child was female, though after the birth she seemed quite bluff about the gender of her eldest and told Charles Locock, her obstetrician, that 'next time it will be a boy'.

'Dear Albert said he had never thought
last year on this day, that his next birthday would
be spent with his dear wife at his side and with
the hopes of a coming child!'

VICTORIA'S JOURNAL, 26 AUGUST 1840

THE QUEEN LOVED the attention Albert showered on her during her early pregnancies – she found it romantic. Motherhood itself she found more contradictory. During pregnancy, Victoria was reluctant to allow doctors to examine her, and Eleanor Stanley, a maid of honour in Victoria's service, describes medical men positioning themselves at the windows of the palace to watch the Queen getting into her carriage so they could guess how far gone she was. The truth was that medical knowledge was at such a primitive stage with regard to maternity care that though to the modern reader this seems cavalier on Victoria's part, in fact there was little the doctors could do to either diagnose difficulties or avert them. The best action a pregnant woman could take at the time was to eat a healthy diet and maintain hygiene to prevent potential problems rather than cure them.

SIR ROBERT PEEL:
I am glad, Ma'am, to see you fully recovered. How fortunate you are to have such an able substitute.

ALBERT:
I try to be of service.

Left: Queen Victoria with Prince Albert in 1854.

PERSONAL HYGIENE

THE VICTORIAN ERA was filthy by modern standards. The well-known maxim 'Cleanliness is next to Godliness' was coined by the preacher John Wesley in 1778, but London had certainly not taken his words to heart. The upper classes generally bathed only a few times a month (and the lower classes even less frequently) and usually not at home. Instead, they headed to the Turkish baths that had become popular from the 1850s, particularly among upper-class men. By the end of Victoria's reign over 600 Turkish baths had been built across the country. For women, costly bathhouses offered arsenic and lime washes to chemically burn off body hair if they did not want to shave, as the vogue for sleeveless evening gowns meant that upper-class women had to depilate.

Victoria herself was erratic in her personal hygiene and was told off on one occasion by Lord M for not having had a bath. Several visitors to court reported kissing the Queen's jewel-bedecked hand and noticing that her nails were grimy.

Dentistry was also in its infancy. The French physician Pierre Fauchard, who died in 1761, is credited with being the father of the science; he pioneered fillings and braces and suggested swilling the mouth with urine to prevent cavities – which would, in fact, have been effective because urine has antiseptic properties. Even primitive dental implants were possible; the poor would sell their teeth to replenish the mouths of the upper classes (who had far poorer dental health because they had more access to sugar). The first toothbrush, however, was not patented until 1857, and as Victoria's reign continued, despite advances in the science, it was still common even for the upper classes to have brown teeth and large gaps!

Head lice and bed bugs were also endemic. In the 1870s, a study suggested that 90 per cent of children had head lice, and these had to be picked out by hand. Victorian manuals suggest wiping sheets with kerosene to kill off bed bugs, while urine was commonly used by the working classes to disinfect clothes and blankets because soap was considered a luxury. For the middle classes, cleanliness became a social indicator and over time was even considered a moral duty, just as Wesley had suggested a century before. Household staff spent huge amounts of time keeping houses clean, as well as their employer's family. The middle classes also instituted family bathtime, and as plumbed water and sewage became part of middle-class life, new products began to appear on the market. 'Hair wash' emerged from the 1830s onwards, based on recipes already in use in India, and in the 1850s the first commercial hair dyes became available.

....

Opposite top: a Victorian Turkish bath hot-chamber in Jermyn Street, London. Opposite bottom: Victorian hair dyes.

TURKISH BATHS IN JERMYN-STREET: THE HARARAH, OR HOT-CHAMBER. - SEE SUPPLEMENT, PAGE III.

FOR YOUTHFUL APPEARAN...

BRODIE'S IMPERIAL HAIR DYES, &c.

(Registered No. 64595)   ONE LIQUID.

Harmless, Perfect, Permanent and Odourless, Clear and without Sediment.

No .   BLACK
No. 2. DARK BROWN
No. 3. LIGHT BROWN
No. 4. { GOLDEN BROWN or AUBURN }
No. 5. PURE GOLDEN

No. 6. Imperial Hair Grower

HOW TO COLOUR YOUR HAIR
WITH PERFECT SAFETY

A VALUABLE AID TO PERSONAL BEAUTY

Medical Certificate with each Bottle

BRODIE'S IMPERIAL PREPARATIONS FOR THE HAIR.

PRICES 2/6, 3/6, 5/0 & 10/6 per Bottle.

FORWARDED per PARCEL POST, POSTAGE PAID, securely packed and free from observation, with full instructions.

J. BRODIE & CO., 41, MUSEUM STREET, LONDON, W.C.

'What humiliation to the delicate feelings of a poor woman ... especially with those nasty doctors.'

VICTORIA ON CHILDBIRTH, 27 JULY 1860

VICTORIA:
The birth was so distressing and nothing has become easier since.

WHILE VICTORIA AVOIDED medical attention, royal pregnancy and births were the subject of much ceremony and tradition, which had to be honoured. Eight of Victoria's nine children were born at Buckingham Palace. Royal births traditionally took place in a very public fashion, with ministers, privy councillors, bishops and ladies-in-waiting all in attendance, because for many centuries there had been fears that royal babies might be swapped with 'pretenders' – babies from other families smuggled into the succession. Each royal birth was potentially the birth of a British monarch, so no chances were to be taken and it was therefore vital that lots of witnesses were present. Albert got rid of these bystanders although many royal office holders now simply attended the palace and waited outside the birthing room, rather than being present for the actual event itself.

Albert, however, broke with tradition. He protected Victoria by ensuring that staff did not talk about what was happening over the course of her pregnancy and he did not make the expected formal announcements about the progress of his wife's condition. Many courtiers complained that they simply didn't know what was going on. Albert also challenged tradition by attending the births of his children. Victoria's first child, the Princess Royal, took twelve hours to appear and the Queen admitted that she 'suffered severely' at the birth. She later wrote that 'there could be no kinder, wiser nor judicious nurse' than Albert. He was clearly upset by her distress and sought pain relief on his wife's behalf, but it would be more than a decade before Victoria was finally granted access to chloroform, to be administered as an anaesthetic.

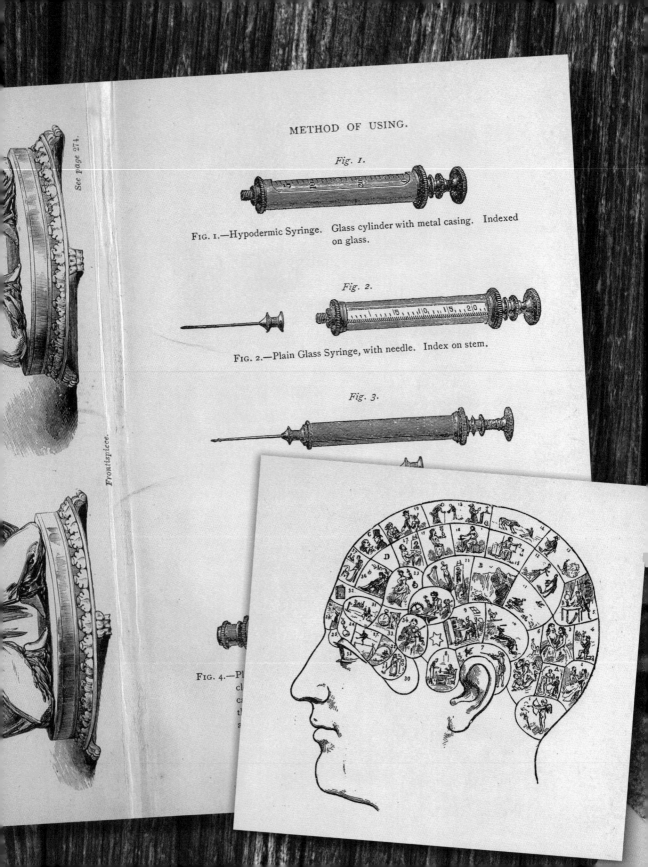

See page 274.

Frontispiece.

METHOD OF USING.

Fig. 1.

Fig. 1.—Hypodermic Syringe. Glass cylinder with metal casing. Indexed on glass.

Fig. 2.

Fig. 2.—Plain Glass Syringe, with needle. Index on stem.

Fig. 3.

Fig. 4.—Pl

VICTORIAN DRUG USE

IN THE VICTORIAN era many drugs that are illegal today were commonly available, including cocaine, opium and marijuana, which were all used in household remedies, prescription and patent medicines. Women were often supplied with such drugs for 'female complaints' like menstrual cramps, pregnancy and neuralgia. One of the palace physicians, J. Russell Reynolds, was known to widely prescribe cannabis for various complaints, including period pain, and it is likely that he suggested the Queen try cannabis for this reason. Victoria hated the smell of tobacco smoke and banned the practice from her court, so if she did take cannabis it is most likely that she drank a tincture or tea made from the seeds.

There is also evidence that Victoria tried Vin Mariani. This was a Bordeaux wine or claret infused with coca leaves (from which cocaine is derived). It was a highly popular tonic and garnered testimonials from Jules Verne, Pope Leo XIII, the famous inventor Thomas Edison and the actress Sarah Bernhardt. Empress Elisabeth of Austria used cocaine for period pains.

As well as cocaine-based tonics, laudanum (or opium) was also widely available. The poet Elizabeth Barrett Browning used tincture of opium and had done from the age of fourteen. 'The tranquilising power has been so wonderful,' she wrote to her husband, Robert. She often said the drug helped her to be more productive. Sarah Bernhardt was also known to use laudanum to help her perform when she was ill.

As well as hard drugs, folk remedies and quack diagnostic techniques abounded, including phrenology – a craze that swept London in the 1840s that involved reading the skull for character traits and medical information. At least phrenology couldn't actually cause any harm, unlike some of the Victorians' wilder remedies. Medical dictionaries of the day, for example, suggest a mixture of warm, soapy water and gunpowder be ingested to cure stomach ache. Pipe ash was thought to cure wasp stings and hanging a dead mole around the neck of a teething baby was said to alleviate their toothache. Some remedies included actual poisons – Munyon's Grippe Medicine, recommended for flu, was a combination of sugar and arsenic. One of the era's less harmful remedies was Negus, a hot drink often taken at bedtime to help alleviate stress. It was made of port, sugar, lemon, nutmeg and hot water – and we know Victoria enjoyed it.

The Queen's medicine chest is still on display at Osborne House to this day and thankfully does not contain any of the more dubious remedies on the market. Over the course of her reign there were huge advances in medical practice, but in the second series we see how some archaic practices were still very much in use, such as Lord Melbourne being bled with leeches. This treatment was only abandoned in the mid nineteenth century – a good decade into Victoria's reign – and would not have helped Melbourne recover from the strokes he suffered latterly.

Killer diseases such as cholera, smallpox and tuberculosis were rife when Victoria took the throne, and though mortality rates slowly improved throughout the century, in the 1840s working-class men lived on average only into their twenties. Middle-class men fared a little better, with an average life expectancy of forty-five, but the fact was there was little doctors could do in the case of acute illness, and it wasn't until well into the twentieth century that medical treatment truly became effective.

....

Opposite top: A hypodermic syringe used to administer morphine (opium). Opposite bottom: Phrenology study – an 1840s craze that involved reading the skull for character.

VICTORIA:
What does the
Archbishop know
about the pain and
peril of childbirth!
The ignominy
of having to kneel in
front of that old man
as if I had committed
some sin, instead of
having a baby!

AFTER GIVING BIRTH the Queen was expected to spend several weeks recovering before attending a 'churching' ceremony to welcome her back into court life. Though she was the Head of the Church of England, Queen Victoria was not overtly religious. However, we do know that she prayed in private to thank God that she'd survived the births and that all her children were delivered safely. Ultimately, it was a cause of wonder among her subjects that Victoria produced nine children who all survived to adulthood – an almost unheard-of feat at a time when mothers commonly lost over 30 per cent of their children to disease in infancy. In 1839 it was estimated that half the funerals held in London were of children under ten years of age; being a child was even more dangerous than being a mother. Victoria's children were lucky, though, and once safely delivered, they were handed straight over to a wet nurse for breastfeeding. These women were treated well – Princess Victoria's wet nurse was paid £1,000 and given a pension of £300 a year (around £150,000 in today's money).

....
Right: Painted by Franz Xaver Winterhalter, this 1846 family portrait was purportedly one of Victoria's favourite paintings of the prince.

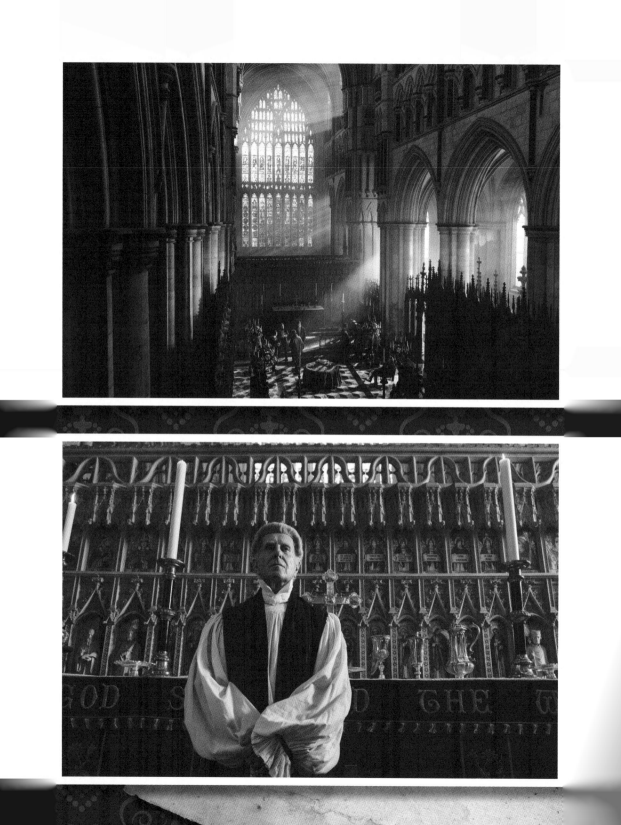

CHURCHING CEREMONY

THE CHURCHING CEREMONY was an ancient religious ceremony to bless a woman after childbirth that by Victorian times had been practised after royal births for centuries. Women were required to come to church decently dressed, which traditionally meant wearing a veil as a symbol of modesty. The service gave thanks for the mother's safe delivery (even if the child was stillborn) and welcomed them back into the community. Churching marked the end of a woman's 'lying-in' time, when she might be confined for a period after the birth to recover – often about forty days. For royal women and particularly for queens, giving birth was a duty to their family and to their country, and royal churching ceremonies reflected this. It's not surprising that she found churching old-fashioned and resented the fact that it highlighted her function as a royal 'milk cow'.

VICTORIA:
I should be pleased,
I know, but it's too
soon. I feel like I am
going back to prison.

INFORMATION ABOUT VICTORIA's pregnancies is hampered by the fact that, after she died, the Queen's diaries were heavily edited by her daughter, Beatrice, and it's impossible to tell what details may have been removed. Still, in this early period, the diaries show no sign of Victoria's later despairing and negative approach to pregnancy and childbirth. In fact, she declares herself quite charmed by the novelty of this new experience and was extraordinarily devoted to her firstborn, Princess Victoria, whom she often kept next to her throughout her working day. George Anson, Albert's private secretary, noted that 'the Queen interests herself less and less with politics . . . and . . . is a good deal occupied with the Princess Royal'. As the years went by, Victoria restricted her time with her children to two visits a day.

After the birth of her second child, Albert Edward, the Prince of Wales, Victoria did not write in her diary for several weeks. When she finally put pen to paper, almost a month after he was born, she expressed feelings of despair and misery, admitting that she had been 'feeling rather weak and depressed' and that she was 'suffering so from lowness'. Many years later the Queen would write to her daughter, 'I own it tried me sorely; one feels so pinned down … our sex is a most unenviable one.' It is quite probable Victoria was suffering from postnatal depression. She was a woman who loved punctuality and order, and the nature of bearing children left her feeling alarmingly out of control.

'When I think of a merry, happy, and free young girl … and look at the ailing aching state a young wife is generally doomed to … which you can't deny is the penalty of marriage …'

~LETTER FROM VICTORIA TO HER DAUGHTER,
PRINCESS VICTORIA, 16 MAY 1860

Opposite: The sixth, seventh and eighth
of Victoria and Albert's children:
Louise, Arthur and Leopold.

TIMELINE OF
VICTORIA'S
BIRTHS

21 NOVEMBER 1840
Victoria, Princess Royal

9 NOVEMBER 1841
Albert, Prince of Wales

25 APRIL 1843
Princess Alice

6 AUGUST 1844
Prince Alfred

25 MAY 1846
Princess Helena

18 MARCH 1848
Princess Louise

1 MAY 1850
Prince Arthur

7 APRIL 1853
Prince Leopold

14 APRIL 1857
Princess Beatrice

HARRIET, DUCHESS
OF SUTHERLAND:
It is easier for a
man. But for us –
having a baby is
a sacrifice as well
as a blessing.

VICTORIA'S STATE OF mind wasn't helped by the closeness of her first two confinements and also her physical size – the heir apparent, in particular, was a large baby and this put pressure on the Queen, who, at under five feet tall, would have found such a pregnancy extremely uncomfortable. Indeed, she later complained of just that, remembering the 'aches … and sufferings and plagues …' It is also likely that Victoria's difficult relationship with her own mother meant she felt overwhelmed by the enormity of the task of motherhood and by her feelings of love for her children. The differing attitudes evidenced in the Queen's journal and correspondence are consistent with bouts of postnatal depression, which severely altered her outlook on the difficult and dangerous business of bearing children from the birth of the Prince of Wales onwards. Reading what she wrote, it is easy to believe that, had contraception been available, Victoria would have stopped after her first two children. However, no such help was at hand.

Thus Victoria came to despise being pregnant and giving birth. She called these 'female duties' the '*Schattenseite*', or shadow side, of her marriage and often compared them to something animalistic or bestial, saying she felt 'more like a rabbit or a guinea pig than anything else'. The issue of loss of control did not only refer to the physical side of childbearing; during her confinements Victoria also lost control of her royal duties. Albert was duly appointed Regent and took over from her during the more advanced stages of her pregnancies until well after the births themselves. A few months after the birth of the Prince of Wales in November 1841, Victoria's spirits were so low that Albert arranged to take his wife to Scotland for a few weeks to give her a break (see pages 200–1). The trip by sea and the subsequent holiday visiting Scottish nobles, particularly her new Mistress of the Robes, the Duchess of Buccleuch, who quickly became a firm friend, seems to have restored the young Queen, who came home to Buckingham Palace and shouldered her duties as a wife, mother and queen once more. However, after only a few weeks it was clear that she was pregnant again. While she continued to enjoy her children (particularly as they grew older – Victoria did not much like babies), she objected strongly to the trials of such frequent pregnancies.

'I am really upset about it and it is spoiling my happiness; I have always hated the idea and I prayed to God night and day to be left free for at least six months, but my prayers have not been answered and I am really most unhappy.'

~LETTER FROM VICTORIA TO ALBERT'S STEPMOTHER,
THE DOWAGER DUCHESS OF SAXE-COBURG AND GOTHA

In essence, Victoria was caught between the traditional feminine role of wife and mother, and her public life as queen. Ultimately, though, her role as queen was more important to her sense of self than her role as a mother. As she continued to fall pregnant again and again, she felt frustrated at being ripped away from what she wanted to be doing. On a personal level, this was the same dilemma that meant Albert, as Victoria's husband, was her 'master' but conversely also her 'subject'. Victoria and Albert were not only man and woman, husband and wife, but also queen and consort. She was aware of this dilemma and commented in her diary that 'good women … must dislike these masculine occupations'. And yet she was the Queen and as such was not comfortable giving up her royal role or power. It was deeply contradictory. The situation would probably have been intolerable if she hadn't loved Albert so deeply and the bond between them had not been so strong. While Victoria had proved herself a competent political player more than able to reign, Albert had proved himself an excellent consort, who had his wife's and children's best interests, as well as the concerns of the country, at heart. There is some suggestion that he enjoyed Victoria's confinements, as they gave him more power to make decisions, but Victoria and Albert were, above all, a formidable *couple*, more powerful together than they could hope to be separately.

ALBERT:
She has changed
so much since the
baby. It has made me
so happy to be
a father, but Victoria
seems almost
to resent being
a mother.

DIANA RIGG
PLAYS
DUCHESS OF BUCCLEUCH

'This Duchess is fictional. Buccleauch is stuck in her ways – very proper, conscious of protocol and standards and she doesn't like the Germans very much, which is very amusing because she's surrounded by them. She's very English and tells it as it is. She would appear to be very proper but there is a little twist in the story where she shows great understanding of a situation that you wouldn't think she would understand.'

THE DUCHESS OF
BUCCLEUCH

'. . . an agreeable, sensible, clever little person.'

···· VICTORIA ON THE DUCHESS OF BUCCLEUCH ····

CHARLOTTE, DUCHESS OF Buccleuch, became Victoria's Mistress of the Robes in 1841, taking over from Harriet, Duchess of Sutherland. The role of Mistress of the Robes was a political one – when a new government came to power, a new Mistress of the Robes was appointed – always chosen to be of the same political persuasion as the ruling party. Victoria had found this tradition difficult to accept in 1839 during the famed Bedchamber Crisis just after she came to power. She refused to dismiss her ladies and replace them with women chosen by the new Prime Minister. So when the government changed from Whig to Tory after Lord Melbourne's resignation, Charlotte was appointed by Victoria on the recommendation of the new prime minister, Sir Robert Peel.

In the series, Charlotte is portrayed by actress Diana Rigg as a much older, curmudgeonly character. However, Victoria and the real Charlotte were contemporaries and there is no suggestion that the Duchess was anything other than light-hearted and supportive in her relationship with the Queen. Charlotte helped Victoria to prepare for her visit to Scotland in 1842 when Prince Albert took his young wife away for a holiday in a bid to lift her post-natal depression. The Duchess of Buccleuch and her husband met Victoria and Albert at Dalkeith during the trip, where the Duke and Duchess had built a church for the local community. With extensive property in Scotland, the Duchess also supported many Scottish charities.

When Charlotte resigned in 1846 because the Conservative government lost to the Whigs, the post returned to the Duchess of Sutherland. Charlotte, however, remained in correspondence with Victoria, and much later in the Queen's reign the same post would be filled by Charlotte's daughter-in-law, Lady Louisa Hamilton.

CORSETS

WOMEN'S FASHIONS IN the Victorian era are defined by one article of clothing – the corset. Corsets formed female bodies into what was considered the perfect silhouette, though the definition of this shape changed over time. Early in Victoria's reign the ideal was considered a 'cone' shape, but by the 1850s the more traditional 'hourglass' had come into vogue. Corsets were originally made by skilled seamstresses, who constructed them from different pieces of material held together by lacing, adding whalebone strips to give support. A 'busk' or piece of wood (or sometimes metal) could be inserted down the centre front of the corset to give a smoother line. Later, the whalebone was replaced by steel strips, which were cheaper and more flexible.

Studies of Victorian women's clothing preserved in museums have shown that women were on average smaller than they are today – in both height and girth. The young tended to wear their corsets tight, with older women allowing themselves more room to breathe! Most women only 'tight-laced' on formal occasions. Corsets came in a variety of shapes to accommodate different activities, including horse riding and pregnancy. While tiny waists were valued highly (Victoria had a twenty-two-inch waist on her Coronation Day), many corsets also had padding in the breast area to provide the 'heaving' bosom that was the natural corollary of the tiny waist.

With the advent of the sewing machine, the corset industry grew: production speeded up, turnover increased into millions of pounds and corsets became more effective and elaborate. Skirts widened and in the 1850s the 'crinoline craze' swept the nation, so it soon became impossible for a fashionable woman to get dressed without the assistance of a skilled lady's maid. Later in Victoria's reign the shape of skirts changed again and 'bustles' came into fashion. Towards the end of her reign, in the late 1870s, what's known as the 'Natural Form Era' defined a more 'natural' silhouette shape as the ideal – though this was still corseted. High heels were also popular in this era to give the impression of a longer leg as the corsets inched lower, binding the upper hips as well as the torso. This style of bodice was known as the 'cuirass' because it felt like wearing an armour breastplate.

....

Opposite: Cinched in; an illustration and newspaper advertisement of late Victorian corsets.

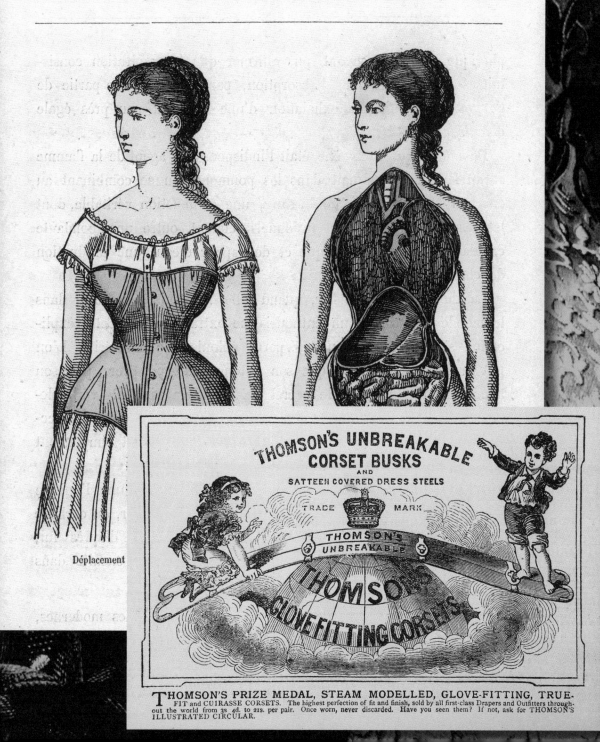

Déplacement

THOMSON'S UNBREAKABLE
CORSET BUSKS
AND
SATTEEN COVERED DRESS STEELS

TRADE MARK

THOMSON'S
UNBREAKABLE

THOMSONS
GLOVE FITTING CORSETS

THOMSON'S PRIZE MEDAL, STEAM MODELLED, GLOVE-FITTING, TRUE-
FIT and CUIRASSE CORSETS. The highest perfection of fit and finish, sold by all first-class Drapers and Outfitters through-
out the world from 3s. 4d. to 21s. per pair. Once worn, never discarded. Have you seen them? If not, ask for THOMSON'S
ILLUSTRATED CIRCULAR.

CHAPTER 4

RAISING A ROYAL FAMILY

'They say no Sovereign was ever more loved than I (I am bold enough to say), and this [is] because of our happy domestic home and the good example it presents.'

···· LETTER FROM VICTORIA TO LEOPOLD, KING OF THE BELGIANS, 29 OCTOBER 1844 ····

WHILE VICTORIA BORE the brunt of pregnancy after pregnancy, Albert took an interest in the royal nursery. He was a new kind of father, ahead of his time, and loved nothing more than rough play and high jinks with his children. Lady Lyttelton, Lady Superintendent of the Royal Nursery, recalled him playing with the Princess Royal. 'Albert tossed and romped with her, making her laugh and crow and kick mightily,' she wrote. Victoria also took an interest in her children, taking the infants Victoria and Albert with her for a daily carriage ride and showing off her progeny to visitors at court. The Queen had a special 'nursery' coach built especially to accommodate the youngsters on longer journeys – down to Windsor Castle or on holiday.

ROYAL PETS

VICTORIA AND ALBERT loved their pets and kept several of them. Dash, Victoria's King Charles spaniel, which features in the series, was one of her real-life favourites. The little dog was given to Victoria when she was thirteen years old and featured often in her diary as 'dear sweet little Dash'; she even made little outfits for him. In November 1834, when Victoria was on holiday at St Leonards-on-Sea, she went driving with her mother, Lady Flora Hastings, Baroness Lehzen and Dash. When one of the horses stumbled, Victoria saved Dash by jumping from the carriage and 'ran on with him in my arms calling Mama to follow'. Luckily, two passing gentlemen cut the horses free, while the ladies, and Dash, took shelter.

Victoria was devastated when Dash died in 1840 (earlier than is depicted in the series). She had him buried at Adelaide Cottage in Windsor Home Park. A marble statue of the little dog was placed on the grave with a loving inscription:

> Here lies
> DASH
> The favourite spaniel of Her Majesty Queen Victoria
> In his 10th year
> His attachment was without selfishness
> His playfulness without malice
> His fidelity without deceit
> READER
> If you would be beloved and die regretted
> Profit by the example of
> DASH

Right: The Princess Royal with Prince Albert and Eos. Opposite: The young family with their beloved canines.

ICTORIA ALSO OWNED a parrot called Lory, which was given to her as a gift by her uncle, the Duke of Cumberland, in 1836. Other favourites were Nero (a greyhound) and Hector (a deerhound), which were painted by Edwin Landseer in 1838. She also owned several horses, ponies and a variety of other dogs, including dachshunds, pugs, collies, hunting dogs and a poodle called Neptune, acquired in 1842. And it didn't stop there. She was also gifted a pair of Tibetan goats by the Shah of Persia when she came to the throne, which were kept in Windsor Park, where they were bred into a herd.

Prince Albert's greyhound, Eos, named after the Greek goddess of the dawn, was his own childhood companion from his days at Rosenau. Eos was painted several times by Landseer and Albert even commissioned Edmund Cotterill at Garrard's jewellers to make him a model of the dog. He described Eos as 'very friendly if there is plum-cake in the room … keen on hunting, sleepy after it, always proud and contemptuous of other dogs'. Always enjoying pride of place in their home, the animals took centre stage over the winter of 1842 and 1843. In conjunction with Garrard's, Albert had been working on an ornate silver-gilt table centrepiece at Buckingham Palace featuring four of the family pets – Queen Victoria's terrier Islay, the Scottish terrier Cairnach, a dachshund called Waldmann and Eos.

When Eos died in 1844, Albert had him buried beneath a mound above the slopes at Windsor Castle. The loss evidently had a profound effect. On hearing of the dog's death, Lord Melbourne declared himself 'in despair at hearing of poor Eos'. And the Queen wrote in her journal, 'Poor dear Albert … He feels it terribly, and I grieve so for him.' In tribute to Eos, Prince Albert had a full-sized bronze statue of the dog by John Francis erected in the grounds of Osborne House in 1845.

ANIMALS

W. C. Fields famously said, 'Never work with animals or children,' but the animals on the *Victoria* set are highly trained and mostly a pleasure to work with. Most have worked in film and television before and come with specialised handlers, who have vans and horseboxes kitted out to keep their charges safe and amused between takes. Each animal has its own personality. Eos, Albert's greyhound, is a lively dog, who loves to run and needs to stretch his legs in between scenes. The dog who plays Victoria's favourite, Dash, is deaf in real life, and was directed solely by hand signals given by her highly skilled trainer.

Everybody wanted to audition the puppy who would play Islay. It was one of the better days on set. Forget the casting couch, the puppy basket is where it's at. Horses come from different suppliers according to their function. In season two of *Victoria*, riding horses, carriage horses and cavalry horses appear in different scenes – or sometimes in scenes together. Actress Jenna Coleman has become quite fond of the large bay she rides in the series.

The animals are rehearsed to familiarise them with what is required, and after a good take treats are given – on days when horses are on set, large quantities of apples are kept to hand. On location it can be difficult to keep the animals at bay – on one shoot at Harewood House, where

some of the Buckingham Palace exteriors are located, horses are not allowed on the grass. So there are no prizes for guessing where most of the horses at Harewood House long to spend their time! The horse master has a busy day on his hands on these occasions, keeping everyone happy – including the animals in his charge.

N THE NURSERY in the new East Wing of Buckingham Palace, the family spoke German and the Queen spent time visiting her children, evidenced by the beautiful sketches and watercolours she drew of her babies, particularly the Princess Royal. The children were also photographed and painted by the leading artists of the day, including Landseer and Winterhalter. Often these pictures included images of the royal pets that were clearly part of the family's day-to-day life, providing a window into the relaxed way Victoria and Albert were happy to see their family represented. Animals are often shown in natural poses and it's easy to imagine the children having fun playing with them. The pictures also chronicle the royal custom of putting both boys and girls in dresses, though the pleating on male and female outfits was slightly different. Great care was taken over the children's wardrobe and layettes and each successive baby had personalised sheets and blankets, monogrammed with their initials in red silk. Their fine cotton baby-caps were intricately embroidered. Later, Victoria took a particular interest in the clothes her burgeoning family wore, choosing sailor suits and kilts for public occasions as a more 'natural' look than the tiny adult-style clothing that children traditionally wore once out of their infant dresses. This started a new fashion in children's outfitting, enthusiastically embarked upon by the middle classes.

DUKE OF SAXE-
COBURG:
Well done, my boy.
A woman like
Victoria needs a brood
of children to
keep her busy.

Right: Victoria, Princess Royal, 1842.

Victoria

VR del. 15/8 1841

THE QUEEN'S SKETCHBOOK

As well as keeping a journal, Queen Victoria kept a sketchbook. This was not unusual in royal circles – her grandfather, George III, was an accomplished draughtsman and so were his daughters, and Victoria's mother, the Duchess of Kent, painted a trompe l'oeil in the conservatory during her time at the Rosenau Palace before Victoria was born.

Victoria was a keen amateur artist who experimented with watercolours, etchings, engravings and drawings. She documented daily life and intimate family moments in these books, which date throughout her life from 1827 to 1890, giving us a historically important glimpse of day-to-day life in the royal palace.

Victoria received drawing lessons twice a week while she was growing up. She called her tutor, Richard Westall, a painter of the Royal Academy, 'a very indulgent, patient, agreeable master'. The young Victoria copied Westall's paintings and was known to give her facsimiles as presents to her mother. Later in life, she often sent her drawings and paintings as gifts or donated them to charity. She once presented a drawing to the United States Embassy in exchange for the writer James Fenimore Cooper's autograph.

At Buckingham Palace, Princess Victoria, or 'Pussy' as the family called her, occupied a great deal of her mother's drawing time in the nursery. The Princess Royal is sketched crawling, being bathed by her nurse, taking her bottle and showing an interest in a caged bird. Victoria's other children appear in her sketchbooks, initially as toddlers, often in back and side views of their outfits to show the detail of the clothing.

Despite her fondness for sketching them, Victoria often criticised her children's aesthetic failings. She liked good looks and hated Bertie's knock knees and the size of his features, especially his nose, which, she complained, 'begins to hang a little'.

Interestingly, Victoria never drew Albert with the children. However, she did take her sketchbook when they went on holiday. When she and Albert first visited Scotland in 1842 she declared that at 'Every turn you have a picture,' and she captured several. She continued to take lessons, including some from artist, author and poet Edward Lear, and, in the longer term, Scottish landscape painter William Leighton Leitch. Under Leitch's tuition she felt she had mastered the potential of watercolour and was greatly excited at her newly acquired skill at capturing light and colour. 'This is very wonderful ….' she enthused. In 1844, when she returned to Scotland, she captured some of the sensuous views around the lodge where she was staying: 'As the sun went down the scenery became more and more beautiful, the sky crimson, golden-red and blue … I never saw anything so fine.'

In later years, however, the Queen's tastes changed. She became more interested in photographs than in making sketches, and her dedication to chronicling her growing family began to wane.

....

Opposite top left: Victoria, the Princess Royal, sketched by her mother, Victoria. Opposite: The Prince of Wales with a parrot, as painted by Victoria.

VICTORIA:
Oh, poor Lehzen.
Was I a terrible
trial to you?

LEHZEN:
The greatest trial
of my life.

FOR HER TIME in the nursery, Victoria had a double apron made, embroidered with her royal monogram, to protect her dresses while she was with baby Victoria – the idea that the Queen was not hands-on is a fallacy, but there is no question that she preferred time alone with Albert to spending time as a family, and that she came to dislike babies once she had given birth to her first few children. Looks were important to Victoria. 'An ugly baby is a nasty object,' she complained in a letter to Princess Victoria in May 1859. When the Prince of Wales was born she noted in her diary, 'Our little boy is a wonderfully strong and large child … I hope and pray he may be like his dearest Papa' – this wish was often repeated in later entries, but almost from the start little Albert was nothing like his father and disappointed Victoria. He wasn't as bright as his elder sister and as his features began to develop the Queen found fault with his looks.

'Lord Melbourne is very glad to hear of the Princess's tooth.'
~LETTER FROM LORD MELBOURNE TO VICTORIA,
17 AUGUST 1841

Victoria frequently wrote to her family and to Lord M about the children's progress and, like any mother, concerned herself with their wellbeing. Her trusted Baroness Lehzen was initially put in charge of the nursery after Princess Victoria was born, despite Albert's objections. There had been tensions between Albert and Lehzen from the start – Albert felt threatened by Victoria's reliance on her old nanny and Lehzen refused to give any ground to Victoria's new husband – but in 1841 an argument blew up between Victoria and Albert that would bring these tensions to boiling point. Princess Victoria, still only a few months old, became ill. Lehzen was nervous of overburdening the child's stomach as she was weaned off her wet nurse's milk, so she ordered a diet of ass's milk, arrowroot and chicken broth. The baby's symptoms were misdiagnosed by James Clark, the royal doctor. We can't say what the Princess was suffering from but the child had lost weight and was fractious, perhaps because of her restricted diet. Lehzen backed Dr Clark's diagnosis, who insisted on the restricted diet and prescribed calomel, a common childhood medicine of the day that contained mercury – now known to be poisonous.

Unsurprisingly, the Princess's condition worsened and Albert blamed Lehzen to the point where he fell out with Victoria when she tried to defend her old friend. Lehzen would not alter her position and refused to accept that she could have taken different decisions. Furious, Albert wrote to his wife, 'I shall have nothing more to do with it; take the child away and do as you like and if she dies you will have it on your conscience.' Ultimately, Victoria gave in and arranged for Lehzen to retire, making public only that the Baroness was doing so for the benefit of her health. Victoria could not bear to say goodbye to Lehzen in person and later dreamed that she had taken the opportunity to do so. She said that waking on the first morning after Lehzen had left was 'very painful to me'.

VICTORIA:
I wish it didn't have to be like this.

LEHZEN:
So do I, Majesty. But I have known ever since you met the Prince that one day you would have to choose between us.

Left: Baroness Louise Lehzen.

DANIELA HOLTZ

PLAYS
BARONESS LEHZEN

'When Victoria met Prince Albert, the three of them became a fragile triangle. Albert wants to have more power and Lehzen is in his way. In a way, Lehzen is a character who has no friends. She has to make all her decisions on her own, she has got a big responsibility – she's a kind of CEO of Victorian times. She's strong, loyal and bright. She's strict if it's necessary but she has a big heart and loves Victoria dearly.'

BARONESS LEHZEN

'She was a good strategist — she was very smart.'

···· DANIELA HOLTZ (LEHZEN) ····

WHEN VICTORIA FIRST took the throne, she installed her childhood governess, Baroness Lehzen, in the rooms next door to her own. This continued after the Queen's marriage and, much to Albert's displeasure, the private doorway between the two sets of rooms was kept in working order – a mark of how highly Victoria still valued Lehzen's advice and support. Lehzen became a kind of unofficial private secretary at Buckingham Palace and carried the household keys – her signature was required for the payment of tradesmen's bills.

Despite public fears that the 'foreign' Baroness had her own agenda and was too great an influence in the young Queen's life, Lehzen never pushed her influence with Victoria and didn't ask for a pay rise or any other benefit during her time at the palace. Albert, however, firmly disliked her. He called her 'the hag' and remarked that she was 'obsessed with the lust for power' and that she 'regards herself as a demi-god'. He considered the Baroness a servant who had risen above her station, and early in his marriage to Victoria they clashed regularly.

The relationship between Albert and Lehzen was essentially a power struggle for Victoria's loyalty and soured beyond repair, and when Victoria arranged for her to retire from the palace in 1842 following a row over the care of the Princess Royal, the Baroness went to live with her sister in Hanover. Ever devoted, she covered the walls of her apartments with pictures of the Queen. Victoria granted a generous pension of £800 a year (around £83,000 in today's money, enough to run a fairly lavish household) and also gave her a carriage. In turn, Lehzen used her pension to financially support her many nieces and nephews. Victoria wrote to Lehzen every month for the rest of the old woman's life and twice made private visits to her when on royal visits to Germany. When Lehzen became ill and could not leave her bed, Victoria sent the gift of a wheelchair. Poignantly, once when the royal train was passing through her home town, the Baroness turned out to wave to her old charge, but the train did not stop.

Baroness Lehzen died in 1870 at the age of eighty-six, and Victoria paid for a memorial to be raised to her memory in Saxony, where she is buried.

'The chief objects here are their physical development, the actual rearing up, the training to obedience. They are too little for real instruction, but they are taught their language & the two principal foreign languages, French & German, as well to speak as to read ... Besides they are taught the figures & Counting & from their 4th year they receive the elements --of Religious instruction.'

ALBERT'S MEMORANDUM ON EDUCATION IN THE ROYAL NURSERY, WRITTEN IN 1847

ALBERT:
Perhaps, Baroness, they do not listen to you. But I assure you that I have no intention of failing.

WITH LEHZEN GONE, Albert took over the management of the nursery, overseeing every aspect of its running and daily routine. When Princess Victoria recovered, he set about creating an extraordinary educational environment. Albert's programme was gruelling, with Baron Stockmar, the Prince Consort's adviser, noting that the regime would give any child brain fever. Albert ignored this criticism and expected only the very best from his children. In a letter to the Duchess of Saxe-Coburg on 16 February 1843, he wrote, 'There is certainly a great charm, as well as deep interest, in watching the development of feelings and faculties in a little child,' and so he set about developing his children's talents from the start, with a highly disciplinarian routine focused on hard work and obedience. Corporal punishment was common in Victorian times and the royal children were not spared 'a real whipping' if they stepped out of line. Later, if they played a wrong note during piano practice, their fingers would be struck hard. Albert wrote a memorandum about education in the royal nursery in 1847, but had already been putting his ideas into practice for several years by then. When Lady Bloomfield visited the nursery at Christmas in 1842 she reported that 'the Prince of Wales had a cold but he is a dear little boy; and, considering we are all strangers, I never saw such good children. They are not a bit shy.'

'We found our dear little Victoria so grown and so improved, and speaking so plain, and become so independent; I think really few children are as forward as she is. She is quite a dear little companion. The Baby is sadly backward, but also growing, and very strong.'

LETTER FROM VICTORIA TO LEOPOLD, KING OF THE BELGIANS, 20 SEPTEMBER 1842, ON HER RETURN FROM SCOTLAND

THE PRINCESS ROYAL was the nursery's star – an extremely bright child who took to Albert's regime almost as soon as she could walk and who started French lessons at just eighteen months. From early on she also spoke (albeit falteringly) English and German. By the time she was five she had mastered all three languages and could read and write. Not all Victorian families educated their girls on an equal footing with boys, and in the upper classes it was often assumed that, as a girl would marry, there was no need for a formal education. As a result, upper-class girls were taught to draw, arrange flowers and play music so they would be able to entertain their husbands' guests. It was not unheard of in the first part of the nineteenth century for some aristocratic women to be illiterate. However, Victoria and Albert's children would marry into Europe's royal houses and would need to be able to hold conversations with statesmen and politicians as well as to make a contribution to public life. They were tutored in mathematics, geography and Latin as well as foreign languages.

VICTORIA:
Look, Lehzen, she's smiling at me.

BUCCLEUCH:
Wind, most likely.

RAISING A ROYAL FAMILY
···· 125 ····

THE REAL LIVES OF
VICTORIAN CHILDREN

LIFE FOR VICTORIAN children was nothing like the lives of children today, regardless of whether they were born into affluence or poverty, although there's no question that children born into working-class families faced the toughest lives. Child labour was normal; in fact, working-class families relied on the money earned by their children to survive. At the beginning of Victoria's reign children worked in factories, on farms, down coal mines and in service. Small, nimble fingers were prized and young children were often used to sweep Victorian chimneys – by the age of nine or ten they were too large and moved on to other professions. To stop their valuable charges growing, chimney sweeps were even known to starve their chimney boys.

When the novelist and social reformer Charles Kingsley wrote *The Water Babies* in 1863 he brought the plight of the chimney sweeps to public attention and people campaigned against this particularly cruel practice, but the truth is that many children – not just chimney sweeps – lived on starvation wages at the complete mercy of their employers. The kidnapping of children to put them to work was commonplace, and high levels of adult mortality meant that a ready supply of orphans was available to be exploited. Indeed, until the Ten Hours Act of 1847, children could be forced to work incredibly long hours, and in fact, the Act only restricted a child's working day to ten hours.

It's not surprising that childhood illnesses and injuries were common. Diseases that are hardly heard of today thanks to immunisation could be devastating. Measles and mumps, for example, could prove fatal. Rickets and polio were widespread. Cholera and typhoid were endemic for adults and children alike. As public hygiene improved and the sources of cholera and typhoid became understood by scientists, working-class children stood a better chance, but in the early years of Victoria's rule medical knowledge was such that there was only a limited amount doctors could do. In desperation, parents often turned to quack cures that were advertised in newspapers – many of which were extremely harmful.

As for education, in the early part of Victoria's reign schooling was only for the rich, but in 1870 the Elementary Education Act decreed that all children in England and Wales aged five to thirteen were entitled to a basic primary education. While discipline was vicious (boys and girls alike were beaten for infractions) and class sizes were huge (seventy or eighty to a class was not uncommon in inner cities), this did at least educate the lower classes and take children out of the working population until they were teenagers.

Rich children had an entirely different experience. Most were educated at home until the age of ten, when boys were then sent away to school, while girls remained at home. The biggest challenge faced by upper-class children was boredom! Children were expected to behave like mini-adults as soon as they got out of the nursery at the age of six, and toys were generally based around sporting activities. Children today would find the lives of most upper-class children – with no radio, no television, no movies and no computer games to entertain them – extremely tedious.

....

Opposite top: Child chimney sweep.
Opposite bottom: Child labourers working in a coalmine.

'... one ought always to be indulgent towards other people, as I always think, if we had not been well brought up and well taken care of, we might also have gone astray.'

LETTER FROM VICTORIA TO PRINCE ALBERT, 11 DECEMBER 1839

VICTORIA FULLY BACKED Albert's educational plan and would later tell her children that 'none of you can ever be proud enough of being the child of *such* a father who has not his equal in this world'. There was no question that she still vastly preferred Albert to anybody else. Bertie continued to be a disappointment. He found it impossible to concentrate on lessons, and while his elder sister chattered away in English, German and French, he fell badly behind. Later, his tutor, Frederick Gibbs, remembered the Prince of Wales's frequent schoolroom tantrums during arithmetic lessons. 'He became passionate, the pencil was flung to the end of the room, the stool was kicked away and he was hardly able to apply himself at all,' Gibbs complained. No expense was spared on his education. The wages that had been paid to Princess Victoria's nursemaid and wet nurse were doubled for the staff taken on to look after the Prince of Wales. He was, after all, the heir to the throne. Women flocked to apply for these positions, including some titled women, but the Queen chose Mrs Brough, an under-servant from Claremont House, to look after her son. In many senses Albert's every need was catered for and his childhood was full of lavish expense, but his bad temper and inability to apply himself point to a little boy out of his depth and sadly misunderstood. Neither Albert nor Victoria were flexible in what they expected of their son, and the battles of the nursery and the schoolroom would continue into Bertie's adult life as he veered off the rails with startling regularity, drinking, taking mistresses and gambling just like his Hanoverian forebears.

DUCHESS OF KENT:
Babies are so easy to love, but when your children grow up, that is when it is hard to be a mother.

VICTORIA & ALBERT
···· 128 ····

ROYAL CHRISTENINGS

'Our christening went off brilliantly . . .'

LETTER FROM VICTORIA TO LEOPOLD, 6 JUNE 1843

ROYAL CHRISTENINGS WERE grand affairs. Royals wore all their finery, as is evidenced in the paintings of the christenings of Victoria and Albert's children, which show men in military uniform and women decked in fine robes and diamonds. Victoria herself often wore her garter robes. The claim to royal status was closely associated with being a member of the Church of England, so christenings were very important. All of Victoria's children had sponsors (or godparents) from the royal houses of Europe and each christening was a lavish occasion, attended by high society and reported in newspapers and magazines. 'Tickets', or rather invitations, were sent out and had to be presented for entry. One grandee was most annoyed when refused admittance by the guards who didn't recognise him, and he had to ride home in his carriage to fetch his ticket in order to see the Prince of Wales at the font.

The Princess Royal was christened in the Throne Room at Buckingham Palace on 10 February 1841, and the robe that was made for her was used for each successive royal christening. A makeshift altar was set up at the palace and the Queen had a silver-gilt lily font made, which was also used for the other royal babies. The following January – a mere eleven months later – the Prince of Wales was christened in St George's Chapel in Windsor. It was a sunny day and organ music was played as the royal party arrived. It was mentioned by one observer that Victoria looked nervous, and we know the young Queen was possibly suffering from postnatal depression at this time. Nonetheless, the christening was an impressive occasion: Handel's 'Hallelujah' chorus was played during the ceremony, and Victoria wrote in her journal that the day started with 'bells ringing and guns firing' and the celebrations continued until long after the baby was asleep, with a huge cake made by celebrated royal confectioner, Mr Mawditt, which ran to four tiers mounted with silvered princes' feathers.

Then, in the evening, a state banquet took place. Victoria was particularly proud of her new 'wine cooler', which had been filled with punch, which was then decanted into golden cups using a shell-shaped golden ladle. This cooler was said to hold thirty dozen bottles of wine, and one observer mentioned that it looked like a huge golden bath! Victoria later wrote, 'It was quite like in olden times & like what one sees represented on the stage.'

Princess Alice's christening took place on 2 June 1843 in the private chapel at Buckingham Palace, with the Archbishop of Canterbury officiating. On 6 September 1844, Prince Alfred was christened in the private chapel at Windsor Castle; Princess Helena on 25 July 1846 at Buckingham Palace. Wherever the royal children were christened, the service and solemnity were the same; however, as Bertie was heir to the throne, his christening was the most lavish, reputedly costing £200,000, the equivalent of several million pounds today.

....

Opposite: Christening of Prince of Wales in St George's Chapel, Windsor.

ERNST:
Albert has always
had a weakness
for numbers. I had
toy soldiers as
a boy, he had
an abacus.

DESPITE BERTIE'S DIFFICULTIES, Albert's plans for the nursery continued apace. Even the toys ordered for the children demonstrated a certain practicality. In 1845 a receipt from craftsman James Izzard lists miniature wheelbarrows and gardening tools as well as the more traditional choices of tea sets, marbles, kites and dolls. Albert was certainly keen for his brood to understand how to look after themselves as well as tutoring them in languages and other disciplines. When the family began to spend time at Osborne House, he made sure that the young Princes and Princess took cookery and gardening lessons alongside more academic pursuits. Sometimes it seems that nothing the royal children did was simply play – everything was designed to teach them about the world. It was an unusual kind of childhood and Albert was a larger figure in it than Victoria. The main key to the nursery was always in his possession and every night he checked the security arrangements, arriving back at eight the following morning to see that all was well. He usually picked up one of the children on his morning visit and took them to visit 'Mama'.

Right: Portrait of Albert Edward, Prince of Wales by Franz Xaver Winterhalter.

ROYAL NICKNAMES

DESPITE ALL ITS obvious formalities, Victoria's world abounded with playful nicknames. When she was growing up, Victoria was called 'Drina' by her mother and Baroness Lehzen. And Victoria herself always referred to Lord Melbourne affectionately as 'Lord M'. Indeed, her relationship with the Prime Minister was so close that outside the palace she popularly became known as 'Mrs Melbourne' – not all Victoria's subjects, it seems, were respectful of the intimacy between them.

As the royal nursery began to fill up, Victoria and Albert gave all their children nicknames, too. Their eldest, the Princess Royal, was known as 'Pussy', though she clearly didn't like the name, declaring on one occasion, 'I'm not Pussy! I am the Princess Royal!' The heir apparent, Albert, Prince of Wales, was known as 'Bertie', and Prince Alfred as 'Affie'. Princess Alice was known as 'Fatima', while Princess Helena was commonly called 'Lenchen'.

Victoria and Albert themselves were given the 'code' names of 'Joseph' and 'Eliza' by the upper echelons of society. This meant that at dining tables in the know, gossip about the royal couple could be voiced and the servants would not know to whom the diners were referring. It also meant that scandalous comments wouldn't sound quite so treasonous – the Victorians were nothing if not discreet.

It was no coincidence that Joseph and Eliza were commonly servant names – a snobbish reference by the courtiers to the bourgeois habits of the royal couple.

LORD MELBOURNE
Lord M

QUEEN VICTORIA
Eliza

PRINCE ALBERT
Joseph

PRINCESS ROYAL
Pussy

EVEN IN THE EARLY part of their marriage, before they bought Osborne House, Victoria and Albert moved often between royal residences – mostly Buckingham Palace and Windsor Castle, where they liked to go to get away from the dirt and fast pace of city life. They also took several holidays, including an idyllic trip to Walmer Castle in Deal in 1842, where the royal couple walked along the beach, hand in hand, talking to local fisherfolk. Victoria wrote to her Uncle Leopold, the King of the Belgians, that the royal family felt 'like prisoners freed from a dungeon' when they got out of town. When she and Albert moved, the royal nursery moved with them, or, as Victoria put it to her uncle in the same letter, 'our awfully large nursery establishment' came too. This was a huge job for the palace staff – packing and unpacking, ensuring favoured toys did not go missing and that the children's routine was not disturbed. The nursery, it seems, was the centre of everything.

'Our young lady flourishes exceedingly … I think you would be amused to see Albert dancing her in his arms; he makes a capital nurse (which I do not, and she is much too heavy for me to carry), and she already seems so happy to go to him.'

~LETTER FROM VICTORIA TO LEOPOLD,
KING OF THE BELGIANS, 5 JANUARY 1841

When Albert died twenty years later, it's telling that Victoria immediately ran to the nursery, where one of the Queen's dressers, Annie MacDonald, reported that she was 'gazing wildly and hard as a stone'. Victoria sat there grieving until after midnight – perhaps because the nursery was the place where she felt closest to her husband; the place he had contributed most to their personal life. Albert's involvement in the nursery was formative for his children, and in later life, when they spoke about their childhood and the nursery with each other, the royals did so in English but with a German accent – a tribute to their father.

ALBERT:
I believe you are tired, Victoria. Your mother was right. You should have taken more time to rest.

CHILDREN

Just beyond the frame of any shot of children in the series, a line of chaperones, nannies and parents sit, out of sight, ready to jump in and comfort any child who might get upset. It takes longer to shoot scenes that involve children for this very reason – there are often stops and starts as mums, dads and carers bounce on set to reassure their offspring. One of the assistant director's favourite tricks to keep the atmosphere light around the younger children is to blow bubbles. It doesn't always work – one toddler who brought a nanny with her was particularly tricky to settle, so the team dressed the nanny in a Victorian nursery maid's uniform so that she could keep the child happy. You can actually spot her slipping in and out of shot in one of the nursery scenes.

The second series of *Victoria* features several children of different ages: in the royal nursery, in street scenes and on location in the Irish Famine scenes. Unlike in Victorian times, working practice for children is now highly regulated, especially in the film industry. Each child is licenced by their local authority and has a designated chaperone, who keeps track of the hours they have been on set and sees to the child's welfare. Children under two can only work for five hours a day and for no more than twenty minutes at a time. Over the age of two, the number of hours goes up, but regular breaks are still a feature and the backstage team work hard to ensure that all child actors are relaxed and

enjoying themselves, with younger children often told they are 'going to a party'.

The baby who played Princess Victoria at six months of age is actually actress Jenna Coleman's goddaughter, but many of the children chosen are twins, so that if one child is finding a scene difficult, the other can step in. Sometimes the children are left on set to play by themselves – several shots are quite natural, just kids having a good time!

In the make-up truck, little girls are given ringlets the old-fashioned way, by tying strips of rag into their hair and twisting the hair around them. Make-up for all children is kept to a minimum.

By the age of five, most kids realise that they are acting and the team carefully familiarise them with the set. Child actors have their own room for breaks and also, sometimes, for tutors, who ensure that no school work is missed. As the series is shot out of sequence, there are often different versions of the same character on set at the same time – a baby Bertie could easily meet his toddler self in the children's room.

Children are cast for a variety of reasons, but for the royal nursery, those who look like Victoria's own sketches are usually chosen, much to the children's delight when they spot themselves in pictures around the set!

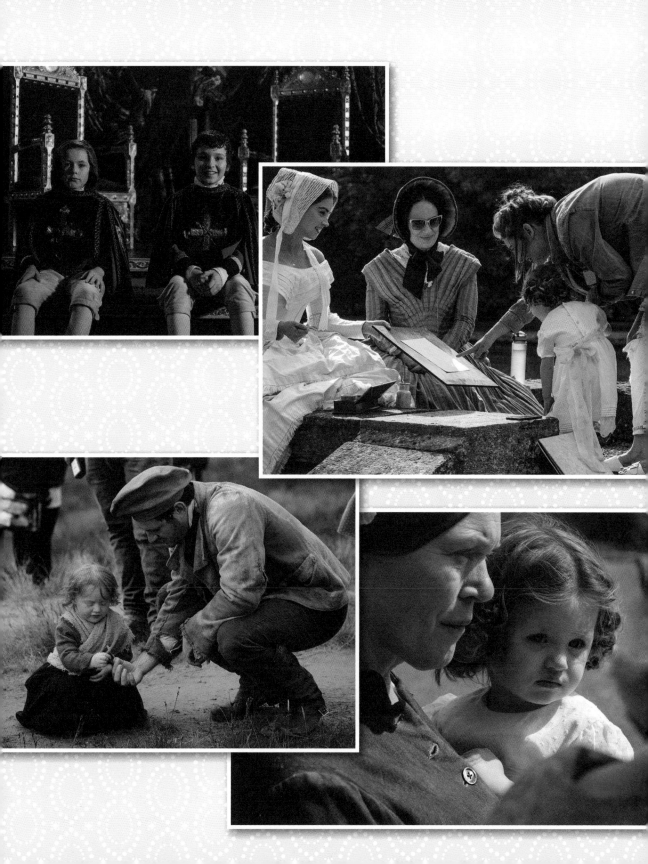

CHAPTER 5
AT HOME WITH VICTORIA & ALBERT

'We all have our trials and vexations but if one's home is happy, then the rest is comparatively nothing.'

···· LETTER FROM VICTORIA TO LEOPOLD,
KING OF THE BELGIANS, 14 DECEMBER 1843 ····

I N THE CENSUS of 1841, Victoria, Albert and the Princess Royal are listed as living at Buckingham Palace along with a long string of staff, servants and courtiers. Victoria's entry simply says 'The Queen', with no occupation stated. The palace had been in the royal family for generations by the time Victoria went to live there, having been developed into a royal residence by George III, and she and Albert were determined to make this sprawling 700-room palace into a modern home and to create as normal a family life as possible – both for them and for their children. To ensure the palace could accommodate their family plans they renovated it again to provide more nursery space, playrooms, schoolrooms and bedrooms through the addition of the East Front in 1847 – the newest of the four wings that surround the courtyard, forming the palace's famous façade.

BUCKINGHAM PALACE

'I wanted to put in as many staircases as possible because they make the dresses look really beautiful . . .'

MICHAEL HOWELLS, PRODUCTION DESIGNER

THE ROYAL FAMILY'S most famous palace began life as Buckingham House, a large townhouse built in 1703 for the Duke of Buckingham. The house was later developed by George III into a royal residence, and then George IV, who employed the foremost architect of his day, John Nash, to spend around half a million pounds on enlarging the building in the 1820s. The house still had its flaws, however. By the time George died in 1830, the house was still not furnished, and Nash did not relocate Buckingham House's kitchen, which was built over a sewer and was therefore notoriously smelly. When George's brother, William IV, came to the throne, he began to furnish the rooms, often using existing furnishings from other royal residences. In 1834, when the House of Commons burned down, King William offered Buckingham House as a new home for the country's government, but it was turned down, and by the time Victoria came to the throne it had become the official London residence of the monarch.

Victoria and Albert part-funded their own remodelling of the house – by then known as Buckingham Palace. The central balcony from which our present royal family are often seen waving to well-wishers on the Mall was installed by Queen Victoria, who waved off and welcomed troops heading to the Crimean War from this vantage point. The royal couple bought furniture and accessories from the Great Exhibition at the Crystal Palace in 1851 and also reused fittings and china from the Brighton Pavilion, which was emptied when they sold it in 1845. The rebuilding undertaken by Victoria and Albert was the last substantial change to the layout of the by now 775-room palace.

....

Opposite top: Façade of the East Front of Buckingham Palace, built during renovations in 1847 and part-funded by the royal couple.
Opposite middle: The Banqueting Room of the Royal Pavilion at Brighton, from which Victoria and Albert transferred fittings to Buckingham Palace.

11 December 1838

'After dinner [I] told Lord Melbourne how Mama teased me about my drinking wine and told people I drank so much which schocked [sic] him much.'

VICTORIA'S JOURNAL, 11 DECEMBER 1838

ELIZA:
Sounds like an excuse for a party to me.

WHILE THE QUEEN and her family lived in luxury, surrounded by aristocrats and politicians, their family life was not far removed from that of their middle-class subjects. They loved to read, they wrote letters and sketched. The royal children, like their parents, delighted in new inventions like the bicycle and magic lantern and were diverted by piano recitals and theatrical presentations. They also attended church regularly and, among other outings, visited London's parks and went out to shows and circuses. Within the confines of the palace, they played games and sports and all the children learned to ride. As well as these more private family pursuits, Victoria loved dancing and drinking and enjoyed parties. They were a family who loved occasions – no celebration went unmarked, from christenings and birthdays to Christmas and anniversaries – and state ceremonies were a normal part of royal family life. The Trooping of the Colour was, for the children, simply the normal way to celebrate their mother's birthday.

VICTORIAN DRINKS

VICTORIA WAS A woman of tremendous appetite. She loved to eat and drink and considered abstaining from alcohol 'pernicious heresy'. She was not alone – Britain was a nation with an appetite for hard liquor.

If you were working class you probably drank either weak beer or gin. These were the only two alcoholic beverages cheap enough for poor people to afford and were certainly safer than drinking water for most of Victoria's reign. As a result, beer was drunk all day and could be as weak as 2 per cent. Local pubs sprang up in working-class areas and many brewed their own beer and distilled their own gin, which was usually drunk at room temperature, neat or with a little sugar stirred in.

The upper classes had more choice when it came to alcoholic beverages. During the early part of Victoria's reign, wine, champagne and brandy had to be bought in cases and were the preserve of the wealthy, though in the 1860s it became legal to buy a single bottle at a time. Mixed drinks were also popular, especially punch, which was regularly served at Buckingham Palace on special occasions. More fancy mixes like cocktails came to Britain directly from America. When Charles Dickens toured the US in 1842 he gleefully partook of Gin Slings, Mint Juleps, Sherry Cobblers and Sangree (Sangria). He wrote about the Sherry Cobbler in his 1843 novel *Martin Chuzzlewit* and smart Victorian society immediately adopted the cocktail – drinking it through a straw was considered highly glamorous. As ice became more widely available, the vogue for cocktails spread and by the end of Victoria's reign upmarket cocktail bars began to appear

in London, including the American Bar at the Savoy Hotel, which opened in the 1890s. A number of books containing cocktail recipes also sold well in the period, from which it can be deduced that the Victorian public liked to make cocktails at home, too.

Victoria's favourite tipple, however, was whisky. William Fraser of the Brackla Distillery obtained a Royal Warrant from Victoria's father, which Victoria renewed in 1838, shortly after coming to the throne. The Queen was not loyal to one particular distillery, however. In 1841, on the eve of the Prince of Wales's christening, a member of the Royal Household wrote to Daniel Campbell of Islay to ask if he might *'procure for the Queen's cellar a cask of your best Islay Mountain Dew'*. It must have gone down well. In a subsequent letter 'another batch of the best Islay whisky for Her Majesty's Establishment' was ordered. Victoria was known to take whisky in her tea and also liked a glass of claret and whisky as a nightcap.

In 1848 the royal family took possession of Balmoral Castle, near the Lochnagar Distillery, and the owner, William Begg, who had sent a card of welcome to the Queen and her family, was delighted when Victoria, Prince Albert, two young princes and a princess turned up on his doorstep the next day. He eagerly showed them round and the Queen and Prince Albert tasted his wares, which then became a firm favourite not only at the family's holiday home in the Highlands, but also at Buckingham Palace.

....

Opposite: A nation with an appetite for alcohol; barrels of locally brewed beverages.

No. 2.

GRAPES destroyed to make WINES & SPIRITS

GIN BRANDY WHISKY RUM

PORT SHERRY

LUNCHEON BAR

G.C.K

PORTER ALE STOUT

Strychnine oil of Turpentine

Wheat destroyed to make GIN

Grains of Paradise Coculus Indicus NUX Vomica

Barley destroyed to make Beer

THESE are the *Drinks* that are sold night and day,
At the bar of the Gin-shop, so glittering and gay.

9 November 1844

'Bertie's birthday table had been arranged by Albert, who is so really good & kind to the Children & so fond of them. Bertie got several toys, & a flag, in particular, caused him great joy.'

VICTORIA'S JOURNAL ON THE PRINCE OF WALES'S THIRD BIRTHDAY,
9 NOVEMBER 1844

BIRTHDAYS WERE ALWAYS a happy affair. Victoria notes in her journal on the Princess Royal's third birthday: 'We wished each other joy of our darling "Pussy's" birthday, who is such a treasure to us, & we pray for her future preservation, to be a comfort to us all our lives!' When the children were young, such celebrations were small family affairs with a few presents and perhaps a special nursery meal. Later, as they grew older, the celebrations became bigger. In 1846, when the Princess Royal was six years old, she was woken in her bedroom at Osborne House by a band playing under her window. The Princess joined her parents at her 'birthday table' and was presented with several pieces of jewellery and a writing box. That evening, Albert treated the whole family to a magic lantern show, and afterwards the Princess stayed up later than usual and had dinner with the adults. Victoria noted that the little girl stayed at the table till the end.

VICTORIA:
Shall we dance?
After all, it won't
be long before
my dancing days
are over.

'At the Service in the Chapel the Christmas Hymn was extremely well sung by our servants, accompanied by trumpets ("Posaunen") & the Organ, which together have such a beautiful & festive effect.'

~VICTORIA'S JOURNAL, CHRISTMAS DAY 1845

THE ROYAL FAMILY generally spent Christmas at Windsor. Albert is popularly credited with bringing the tradition of the Christmas tree to Britain from Germany, but Victoria's family was also German and Christmas trees had long been a British royal tradition. Victoria's grandmother, Queen Charlotte, was known to bring yew trees inside as part of her yuletide celebrations

Traditionally, Victoria and Albert would decorate their tree together, tying on gingerbread and lighting candles before the children were brought in. It's easy to paint a romantic scene with the young couple flirting as they chose where to place the ornaments. Albert also sent gifts of decorated trees to the local army barracks and the nearby school. There is an anecdote that tells of Lord Melbourne driving past at Christmas and catching a glimpse from his carriage of the royal couple lighting Christmas candles together, and then carrying on his journey alone. It's unlikely to be true, but it certainly illustrates the fact that Albert had well and truly taken over the central space in Victoria's life, which had previously been occupied by Lord M.

In reality it wasn't only Lord Melbourne – the whole country was looking in on the royal couple, and when the *Illustrated London News* ran an engraving of the royal family around the Christmas tree in 1848 at the Queen's Lodge in Windsor Castle, it was the first time most British people had encountered the idea of a whole tree being raised for Christmas, though it was common at the time for mistletoe or even branches of holly or yew to be brought inside. Christmas trees immediately became a sensation and soon almost every house had a fir bedecked with sweets and homemade decorations, the air scented with pine cones.

CHRISTMAS

Creating a Victorian Christmas took production designer Michael Howells and his team months to perfect. 'We knew we would have snow, even before we saw the script,' he admits. The snow on set is in fact finely shredded paper – all of it biodegradable. For outdoor scenes, the ground had to be covered and then the 'snow' applied. Snow on trees required a different process. The team scouted for the location of the outdoor skating scene during one of the country's hottest summers. Howells laughs, 'It was a challenge to recreate the sub-zero temperatures. They built an ice rink and then dressed the snow scene around it. When one of the characters falls through the ice the team arranged a "tank stage" so the scene is shot in two different locations, which were later edited together.

'Creating Christmas we relied heavily on the symbols we knew viewers would want to see. It's all about tradition,' Howells says. 'We researched the way Christmas was – not like today at all – but very much about bringing plants inside – holly and ivy and spruce. All about the passing of the seasons. The result is beautiful – though a lot less glitzy than our modern Christmas.' The team worked on two different briefs – the upstairs 'German' Christmas and the 'English' Christmas below stairs – and huge effort went into researching Victorian yuletide traditions so that everything from the garlanding to the Christmas toys shown on screen is authentic.

The Christmas tree was always going to be a focus. 'It had to be spectacular,' Howells says. 'Christmas is a Pagan Festival, really, and we wanted to capture that. Though boughs of spruce or pine had been used inside royal

residences since Queen Charlotte's days, Albert was so important in establishing the decoration of the Christmas tree as a key part of the way most people celebrate, we focused on that.' The decorations were made to order, including hand-made paper chains and 300 orange pomanders, studded with cloves. The team researched at the Toy Museum in Ilkley, where they rented original Victorian toys and also picked up ideas for designs. The resulting mixture of Jacks in the Box, rocking horses, castles, toy soldiers and toy theatres is absolutely authentic, many made by hand specifically for the episode.

Christmas dinner was also important, and on set the menu for the royal family featured beef, rather than turkey, as was more likely in the period. Though the upstairs shoot didn't feature plum pudding, the team tried to find a way to include this traditional Christmas fare, if only below stairs. 'We never know what will make the final cut,' Howells says, 'so everything has to be perfect. I don't know if our plum pudding made it or not. We also had significant amounts of sugarwork to organise – cake was very important.'

Servants worked particularly hard during the festive season with the house full of guests so their Christmas celebrations took place towards the end of the season, sometimes as the decorations came down on Twelfth Night. 'There would be a party for the servants. We wanted to show holly and particularly mistletoe – an opportunity for a stolen kiss,' Howells says with a smile.

....

Opposite top right: Victorian Christmas card.
Opposite middle and bottom: Scenes of the royal family at Christmas time.

WITH THE SEASON'S COMPLIMENTS.

CHRISTMAS TREE AT WINDSOR CASTLE.—DRAWN BY J. L. WILLIAMS.—(SEE NEXT PAGE.)

CHRISTMAS AT WINDSOR CASTLE.

VICTORIA & ALBERT
···· 153 ····

THE ROYAL FAMILY thoroughly enjoyed Christmas. When Lady Bloomfield visited the royal nursery during the festive season in 1842, she reported that the Princess Royal was 'in immense spirits ... running in a state of childish excitement to show ... two new frocks she had received from her grandmother ... as a Christmas box'. The following year, in 1843, Charles Dickens published *A Christmas Carol*, now an enduring holiday classic, which immediately took the public by storm, with a hard-working family and a miser transformed by the Christmas spirit at its heart. In the same year Henry Cole commissioned the first Christmas card from John Callcott Horsley. This card cost a shilling – expensive for the time – but the idea quickly caught on and the royal children were encouraged to make their own cards, which they then sent to friends and family. The family also adopted the use of the newly invented Christmas cracker, or 'cracker bonbons' as they were known, which originally contained sweets.

Right: a Victorian decorated Christmas tree, popularly credited to Albert as bringing the tradition to Britain from Germany.

WINDSOR CASTLE

ET IN THIRTEEN acres of grounds, Windsor Castle is the oldest occupied castle in the world. Victoria's uncle, George IV, had undertaken remodelling work at Windsor, which came with a huge million-pound price tag. As Albert preferred the country, he enjoyed spending time there and getting out of London, where the air quality was not good and life was busier. Victoria, on the other hand, referred to Windsor Castle as 'dull and tiresome' and said it was like a prison, but she deferred to her husband and they used the castle during the visits of many dignitaries and on state occasions, as well as retreating there several times a year with the royal court.

The castle was not ideally suited to these state occasions, with visitors reporting that they were not always comfortable there – the rooms were small and difficult to heat. The kitchens were more efficient than those at Buckingham Palace, however, and during her reign Victoria made improvements to both the castle and its grounds, building a dairy to serve the castle kitchens and refurbishing the State Dining Room after a fire in the 1850s.

Both Victoria and Albert are buried in the Royal Mausoleum at Frogmore, just a mile or so from Windsor Castle.

IN THESE EARLY years there were some famously cold winters during the royal family's Christmas sojourn at Windsor and the lake at nearby Frogmore House often froze over, enabling them all to go ice skating. Another diversion was to take a ride in their red sleigh – one year they got as far as Slough in it, a trip totalling eight miles there and back. Back at the castle, the traditional royal meal wasn't turkey, but rather an array of different meats that varied from year to year. On one occasion a roasted swan was the centrepiece. Another time there was a boar's head. Typically, the royal family would tuck into around twenty different dishes on Christmas Day. The celebrations continued until 6 January, when a 'Twelfth Cake' was shared – a huge, ornately decorated fruitcake to round off the holiday season. Victoria and Albert's family sensibility and commitment to celebration established the tradition of Christmas as a family holiday that endures to this day.

As well as giving each other gifts, Victoria and Albert were generous with their staff and courtiers. When Princess Beatrice edited her mother's diaries she took out many of Victoria's references to servants as she felt it was not fitting for a queen to take an interest in the lower orders. But Victoria in truth knew the names of all her personal servants and was known to be something of a soft touch, so determined was she to give the people around her the benefit of the doubt. She generously gave away gloves she had worn, as well as items of underwear and nightwear and dresses, to her servants.

Opposite: Snowy scenes at Windsor Castle. Below Victoria and Albert enjoying a sleigh ride.

LANGUAGE IN *VICTORIA*

Before every read-through with the actors I make a little speech: '"Ma'am" to rhyme with "ham", not "smarm"; "Buccleuch" rhymes with "taboo", and "Afghanistan" rhymes with "barn".' Trying to get actors to pronounce words the nineteenth-century way is hard, particularly as we don't always know how words were pronounced (audio recordings came late in Victoria's reign), but when we do know we try to be as accurate as possible. A Victorian aristocrat would pronounce 'either' to rhyme with 'fibre', not 'leaver', and woe betide any actor who forgets this.

I have now got so used to writing in nineteenth-century-friendly language that I would never dream of having Victoria say, 'That looks okay to me,' as the word 'okay' only came into common usage in the twentieth century. But despite my best efforts, the odd anachronistic expression does get past my nineteenth-century filter. At one point a character talks about 'falling pregnant' – Victorian women certainly didn't talk about being 'pregnant', which was a medical term; instead, they found themselves in an 'interesting condition'.

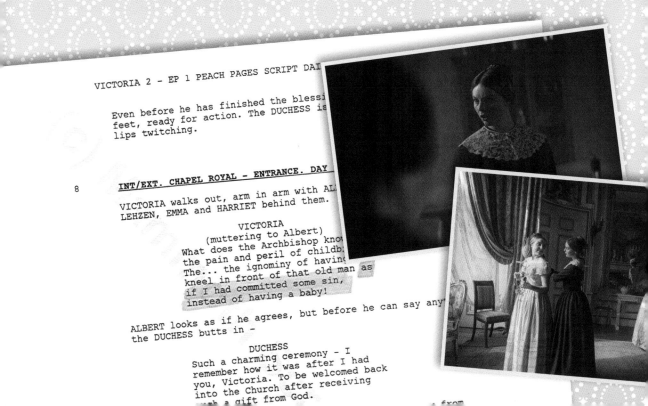

When I am writing an episode I always have the *Oxford English Dictionary* to hand so that I can check when a word or phrase first came into use. It's one of the challenges of writing *Victoria* to come up with language that sounds authentically nineteenth century, but not so convoluted that modern audiences find it off-putting.

The great pleasure of writing nineteenth-century dialogue is finding words and phrases that have fallen out of use: I love the gloriously self-explanatory 'button hole factory' as a euphemism for a brothel, and the word 'transpontine' to indicate someone from South of the River. The Victorian era was a time when educated people would all have known great swathes of poetry and the Bible by heart, so I can have my characters quote Shakespeare or the Old Testament with total credibility. Sir Robert Peel was an Evangelical Christian, so I have peppered his speeches with biblical sayings. And I used the Bible when I was trying to find a way for Wilhelmina to understand the relationship between Drummond and Lord Alfred. The word 'homosexual' didn't exist in the 1840s,

and well-brought-up young ladies would not have been aware that such a thing existed – unless, of course, they had consulted their Book of Samuel, where David's feelings for Jonathan are described as 'surpassing the love of women'.

In reality, Victoria and Albert would often have spoken to each other in German, but as I don't speak German, I decided against making this a feature of the show. Occasionally, though, I have used untranslatable German words such as *träumerei* (literally 'dream state') to show how difficult it is for Albert to express himself in a language that is not his own. And of course his pet name for Victoria is *liebes*, which roughly translates as 'dearest' in English.

Getting the language right is exacting but so important. If a Victorian lady starts talking about getting in touch with her feelings, it's the equivalent of wearing a crinoline with trainers. There is no point in filming by candlelight if the characters communicate in text speak. There are times when I would love for Victoria to say, 'Laters,' but I have to make do with, 'You have my permission to withdraw.'

VICTORIA:
The newspapers
are saying
horrible things.

VICTORIA'S FAMILY LIFE is better recorded than that of any previous monarch – largely due to her collection of photographs, which runs to 20,000 items. The Queen placed such a high value on photographs of her family that before she died she instructed which particular images were to be buried with her. The huge collection includes pictures of royal family life, both posed and candid shots, that show an idyllic childhood of family pursuits. Victoria and Albert would often go through their photographic albums together in the evening. 'It was such an amusement,' Victoria wrote in her journal. 'Such an interest.' While sometimes these photographs can seem formal and give the impression that the family didn't laugh or enjoy themselves, it's important to remember that photographic processes of the day meant that the subjects had to stay still or the image would blur. Most photographs were taken in full sunlight, outside. On some occasions the Queen was not happy with the images, especially her own. 'The day was splendid for it,' she wrote of one session in her journal. 'Mine was unfortunately horrid.' She was known to scratch out her face on the negative or glass plate if she didn't approve of the image.

Victoria and Albert chose to share some of these pictures with the public, making the royal family familiar to their subjects in an entirely new way. Certainly the family were watched eagerly and emulated in all things – even in their dress and accessories. When Queen Victoria wore a Sheffield tortoiseshell comb to the opera one evening, she practically revived the entire industry of British shellware. Similarly, new parents all over the country emulated the names the royal couple chose for the Princes and Princesses. The access the public had to Victoria and Albert was entirely new and it was a risk. Much pomp and ceremony surrounded being royal, and the royal family had up till then always been set apart from their subjects. By sharing even the most common family pastimes, Victoria and Albert succeeded in making themselves more human and easier to relate to, but they also opened themselves to scrutiny and invasion of privacy.

In 1849 the couple caused a scandal by going to court to block the publication of a volume of seventy-four etchings of their family life, which had been stolen by a journalist, Jasper Judge. Judge intended to have the etchings printed and put up for sale. For Victoria and Albert this was a step too far – the images Judge took were relaxed and very private. They show, among other things, the royal children playing with their pets. The book has personal annotations in Victoria's own handwriting. The royal couple won their case in court and Judge was fined. On its return to royal hands, the book was given to George Anson, Albert's personal secretary, and only became public over one hundred years later. This incident shows that the royal couple was in charge of their public persona and, while happy to share their family life to some extent, they understandably wanted to remain in control of what was released to the public and what was not.

....
Above: Photographic portrait
of Queen Victoria, circa 1840.

THE MODERN COOK;

A PRACTICAL GUIDE TO THE CULINARY ART

IN ALL ITS BRANCHES:

COMPRISING,

IN ADDITION TO ENGLISH COOKERY, THE MOST APPROVED AND RECHERCHÉ
SYSTEMS OF FRENCH, ITALIAN, AND GERMAN COOKERY;

ADAPTED AS WELL FOR THE LARGEST ESTABLISHMENTS AS
FOR THE USE OF PRIVATE FAMILIES.

By CHARLES ELMÉ FRANCATELLI,

PUPIL OF THE CELEBRATED CARÊME,
AND LATE MAÎTRE-D'HÔTEL AND CHIEF COOK TO HER MAJESTY THE QUEEN.

WITH SIXTY ILLUSTRATIONS.

TWENTY-FIRST EDITION.

LONDON:
RICHARD BENTLEY & SON, NEW BURLINGTON STREET.
Publishers in Ordinary to Her Majesty.
1872.

A ROYAL APPETITE

THE ROYAL COUPLE had very different attitudes to food. Albert ate solely for fuel and did not relish the lavish spread of dishes that was prepared daily for the royal party's delectation by Buckingham Palace's forty-five kitchen staff. Worse, as far as many men at court were concerned, was that Albert refused to dally 'with the chaps' over port once the ladies had retired at the end of the meal. But he wasn't really a drinker and was not interested in the kind of anecdotes that circulated once the ladies had left and the bottle was being passed from hand to hand – tales of soldiering, sport and infidelity. Many of the royal party were interrelated and had known each other since childhood, and Albert felt left out of their references to long-past incidents. He would leave the table after only five minutes and join the ladies, where he would sing duets with the Queen.

Victoria, on the other hand, relished mealtimes. She became upset if there wasn't a sufficient spread of dishes and complained in her diary that it was a 'miserable day – no pudding'. In her childhood, Victoria's food had been rationed and the young Queen cut a slim figure as a result, but when she took over her own household that swiftly changed and she steadily put on weight. She also ate very quickly, cramming food into her mouth, and although she was aware that this was bad manners and tried to slow down, she didn't succeed. As Queen, when she had finished what she was eating the plates were removed, so if you were at the table and did not eat as quickly, you would not get to finish your meal. And you certainly

had to be fast to keep up – it was said that Victoria could polish off seven or eight courses in as little as half an hour.

Despite the Queen's well-known love of sweets – she enjoyed all kinds of baked goods, especially tarts and cakes, and the wafer biscuits that her Uncle Leopold sent her from Brussels – she also liked savouries. She would pick up bones with her fingers and was very fond of mutton chops, eating them messily without using cutlery. On one occasion, a French visitor watched, open-mouthed, as she demolished three large platefuls of soup. Victoria also loved buttered toast – something a German newspaper had to explain to its readership, describing it as 'slices of bread roasted on the coals and buttered hot'. The Queen ate vast quantities of it.

Victoria often preferred to breakfast privately in her room and then drank a glass of hot water at 10 a.m. to settle her digestion. She also loved to drink, and records show her particular fondness for wine and whisky. There's no question that, unlike her husband, Victoria had a hearty appetite.

AFTER QUEEN VICTORIA'S chef, Charles Elmé Francatelli, left her service at Buckingham Palace on 31 March 1842, he went on to manage kitchens at both Crockford's Club and the Reform Club. Francatelli was of a naturally liberal disposition and wanted to help improve the diet of ordinary people, while cooking for the upper crust. He wrote four cookery books, including *The Modern Cook* and *A Plain Cookery Book for the Working Classes*.

Opposite left: Francatelli's cookbook The Modern Cook.

'Her Majesty confesses to a great weakness for potatoes, which are cooked for her in every conceivable way.'

ANONYMOUS ACCOUNT OF VICTORIA'S FAVOURITE DISHES, 1901

FRANCATELLI:
There was a quart of cream in the pantry last night, for the syllabub tomorrow, all gone. And don't tell me it's rats, Mr Penge. Any more pilfering and I'm going to the Baroness.

THE HANDWRITTEN MENUS embellished with a St George's cross at both Windsor Castle and Buckingham Palace reveal the royal family's favourite foods, including dishes served especially to please Prince Albert (rice pudding – his particular favourite – is sometimes written on the menu in German). Albert was difficult to please at the table – he was more interested in doing things and considered eating a waste of time. Victoria, on the other hand, loved to eat and was known to 'gobble'. She didn't like to linger too long at the table and famously had a sweet tooth, enjoying:

… chocolate sponges, plain sponges, wafers of two or three different shapes, langues de chat, biscuits and drop cakes of all kinds, tablets, petit fours, princess and rice cakes, pralines, almond sweets, and a large variety of mixed sweets … Her Majesty is very fond of all kinds of pies, and a cranberry tart with cream is one of her favourite dishes.

~ *THE PRIVATE LIFE OF THE QUEEN*, BY ONE OF HER MAJESTY'S SERVANTS, 1897

Victoria controlled the menus served in all the royal residences and ordered plain soups and roasts to be served in the nursery, though the children's favourites (like Osborne Pudding – a bread and butter pudding made with brown bread and marmalade) also feature. However, the royal children were allowed and even encouraged to join the adults at mealtimes, dipping in and out of one of the most cosmopolitan dining tables in the world. It would be good preparation for their future lives as kings and queens of Europe.

FOOD

Production designer Michael Howells' team make sure that every prop on set looks perfect – from silk flowers to the huge gilded mirrors in Buckingham Palace – but nothing requires more attention to detail than the food that dresses Victoria's special occasions, from christenings to the Plantagenet Ball to Christmas. One thing's for sure: not everything is as it seems.

The platters of oysters served at the Plantagenet Ball were made out of lychees. 'We need to accommodate actors' allergies and their food preferences,' Michael explains. 'We work very hard on that.' There are also modern-day laws to consider – it's now illegal to eat the tiny birds that were actually served by the King of France when Victoria and Albert visited him in 1843, so Howells' team had 200 tiny marzipan birds created, each one painted individually by hand to look like the real thing.

In many cases, however, the food on set is real. The glamorous ice sculpture of a swan that graced the Plantagenet Ball feast, for example, was in fact two ice sculptures, both made in Cardiff, driven to the set and then swapped around so that they would last the three and a half days of filming under hot studio lights required for the ball scenes. The biscuits, cakes and marzipan on display at the ball were all sourced from local people. 'There are some phenomenal bakers up here in Yorkshire,' Howells enthuses. He worked closely with local companies, referencing the original recipes of Victoria's head chef, Charles

Elmé Francatelli. Unlike in the first series of *Victoria*, in which Victoria and Albert's huge wedding cake was mostly made of plastic, the cakes and puddings at the ball were real. Howells' team also worked with taxidermists on the glorious display of poultry dishes, which included peacocks, swans and geese.

CHAPTER 6
REFORMING THE ROYAL HOUSEHOLD

'We shall never be in a position to occupy ourselves with higher and graver things, so long as we have to do with these mere nothings.'

···· LETTER FROM ALBERT TO BARON STOCKMAR, CHRISTMAS 1842 ····

WHEN VICTORIA CAME to the throne, the royal palaces were luxurious but poorly run. When the Prime Minister of France was a guest at Windsor Castle he reputedly wandered the halls for an hour trying to find his rooms. There was nobody on duty to help and he stumbled upon the Queen at her toilette, having her hair brushed by a maid. The poor man retreated swiftly and eventually, it must be presumed, found the correct bedchamber. This demonstrates just one way in which the royal households were hopelessly managed, and in 1842 Albert took it upon himself to make necessary, if unpopular, changes – both financial and organisational.

Albert's adviser, Baron Stockmar, was a royal financial whizz. He had contributed to the keeping of Albert's father's accounts since 1817 and understood the benefits of the sound financial management of royal affairs. When the Baron visited Buckingham Palace he was shocked at what he saw, and it was natural for Albert to turn to Stockmar when he decided to modernise the royal household. Albert had already tried to speak to the Prime Minister, Sir Robert Peel, about the inefficient way the palaces were run, but Peel did not want to get involved – too much offence was likely to be caused to vested interests, and he considered meddling in palace affairs to be opening a can of worms. 'Men of high rank are eager to hold these offices in the royal household,' he replied to Albert's objections, 'and it will make trouble if anyone is put over them, or if there is any interference.' In other words, the organisation of the palaces was outdated, costly and inefficient, but it was *English*. Albert bided his time.

A DAY IN THE LIFE

VICTORIA AND ALBERT had a set routine each day. The Queen liked to breakfast privately in her rooms but she felt guilty about this, so most days she ate breakfast with close family at Buckingham Palace at nine each morning. Afterwards, the royal couple often walked in the palace's extensive gardens, which Albert had stocked with aquatic birds and animals. The Prince had trained the birds to come when he whistled, just as he and Victoria walked on a bridge across the pond. The couple then worked together for a couple of hours on government business and often spent an hour drawing, during which time their children might visit.

Lunch was served at 2 p.m. and was usually a family meal, with only close courtiers in attendance. The Prime Minister came in the afternoon on most days, and there might also be other official visitors. Around five o'clock Victoria and Albert went out for a ride, either in a carriage or on horseback. Sometimes equerries accompanied them. They liked to ride all over London, often going as far as Hampstead Heath, though some days they restricted their outing to the confines of Hyde Park. Afterwards, back at the palace, they read – sometimes Albert read aloud to his wife, which she enjoyed – and then spent time in the nursery before dinner.

The evening meal was a more public affair. It started at 8 p.m. and usually involved guests, eating with their entourage and any visitors. It was not unusual to sit down with fifty people at dinner. On some occasions the royal children were welcomed to the table and allowed to join in. Princess Victoria in particular was a precocious child and enjoyed the stimulation of adult company.

After dinner, the evening generally included some form of entertainment, either inside the palace walls or in the city. They might go to the opera or theatre, or stay in and play music together. Both adored the music of Felix Mendelssohn and all Queen Victoria's ladies sang. Now and again there would be a large society event, like a ball, and Victoria, of course, loved to dance. In the evenings Buckingham Palace was a lively place, and although the Queen was a night owl while Albert found frequent late nights difficult, it was nonetheless extremely rare for the couple to spend even a single night apart. Ever devoted to each other, the vast majority of their time was passed in each other's company.

....

Opposite top: Buckingham Palace, 1840

WHEN VICTORIA ENQUIRED why there was never a fire lit in her dining room she discovered that the Lord Steward was responsible for laying the fire but the Lord Chamberlain for lighting it. The result was that the Queen ate in the cold. More reports arrived of royal guests left unshepherded in the palace's labyrinthine corridors while staff enjoyed themselves in the back rooms. If a pane of glass was broken, the signatures of five different officials were required before it could be fixed. In the end, Albert ignored Sir Robert Peel's stance and decided to deal with the Royal Household on his own. He did so in a rigorous manner entirely consistent with his personality and spent hours studying the royal accounts and interviewing servants and staff.

The exercise was one way by which Albert could ease Victoria's path, prove his devotion to her and demonstrate his real skills in the areas of organisation and reform. In the early years of their marriage, Albert struggled to find something worthwhile to occupy his time. As issue after issue rose in the domestic arrangements at the palace, he realised that making changes to the running of the Queen's day-to-day life was a task he could undertake that would have a real impact. The work was not only organisational; as he studied the household accounts, Albert realised he could also save huge sums of money, freeing up capital for expenditure on other things. He managed to save £400 a year by rearranging the laundry and an astonishing £25,000 a year by reorganising the pension arrangements for palace staff.

ALBERT:
The wages of Royal servants are uncommonly low. So, it occurs to me that if the wages were higher, the household accounts might become more sensible.

Screenwriter Daisy Goodwin on writing *Victoria*...

PRINCE CONSORTS, THEN AND NOW

The role of prince consort has never been an easy one. To be an alpha male of considerable ability consigned to the distaff occupations of hand-shaking and ribbon-cutting was a problem for Prince Albert, just as it has been for his great-great-grandson, Philip Mountbatten. They were both princes without a portfolio. Albert was the younger son of an insignificant German duke; Philip the youngest child of an insignificant prince, who's father had been parachuted onto the Greek throne.

Both were encouraged to marry the heiresses to the British throne by ambitious uncles. Albert's marriage to Victoria was engineered by the wily patriarch of the Coburg dynasty, Leopold, King of the Belgians, who through some shrewd marriage-broking had made his family the stud farm of European royalty. Philip's marriage to Elizabeth in 1947 was encouraged by his uncle, Louis Mountbatten – another royal princeling who punched above his weight. Both Albert and Philip were noticeably good-looking. Albert was described as the most handsome prince in Europe at the time of his marriage – the photographs of him taken fifteen years later when he was already ill do not do him justice. Philip, of course, had matinée-idol good looks that worked very well on screen – an

attribute that has become increasingly important to the royal family. Both men had traumatic childhoods: Albert's parents separated when he was only five and his mother was forced to leave Coburg and died a few years later in Paris. Philip's mother, Princess Alice of Battenberg, was confined to a psychiatric institution for much of his childhood, and like Albert he learned the hard way from an early age that life was fundamentally insecure, even for a prince.

Philip, of course, has outlived his great-great-grandfather, who died at the tragically early age of forty-two, but both men struggled against the inherently conservative nature of the court. Albert was horrified by the waste and corruption that bedevilled the royal household in the 1840s. A management consultant before such things were even thought of, he swept through the palimpsest of royal perks, making money-saving changes that were not always met with approval by staff (see page 182). Upstairs and downstairs Albert was viewed as a parsimonious foreigner with suspect habits – there was much sniggering at his penchant for thigh-high red boots, for example. Philip met with the same kind of resistance nearly a hundred years later when he, too, tried to modernise the Royal Household. Both men were muttered about in corners as being brusque and having no feeling for tradition. They were also considered to have undue influence over their wives. We can only guess what our current Queen has thought of these suggestions, but we know that Victoria was furious at any criticism of her 'angel', although she herself was not always happy at being advised by Albert. Theirs was a passionate but stormy marriage; it would be hard to imagine Elizabeth throwing a glass of wine over Philip in public as Victoria once did to Albert.

Albert left the template for a prince consort in terms of public works and his legacy can be seen today all over 'Albertopolis', or what we now call the museum district of South Kensington. Philip has left another kind of mark on the nation in the form of the Duke of Edinburgh Awards. It will be up to posterity to decide which has been more significant.

Philip and Elizabeth are both the great-great-grandchildren of Victoria and Albert, and I would argue there is more of Victoria in Philip and more of Albert in Elizabeth. Philip has inherited Victoria's passionate directness, whereas Elizabeth appears to have all of Albert's dutiful seriousness of purpose.

Both couples have had problems with their children, and probably for the same reasons: both Albert and Philip had unrealistic expectations of their offspring. The two consorts may have been very different in character – Albert wrote music and was the royal family's last great collector of art; Philip's interests were more sporting – but each in his own way has shown the dignity and potential of being the husband of the Queen.

....

Top: Portrait of Prince Albert. Right: Queen Victoria and Prince Albert later in life in 1861.

'There is only one truth, as in mathematics . . . for a man of honour there is only the bird's-eye view, standing firmly above the low actions of the world, supported by noble principles.'

LETTER FROM ALBERT TO HIS BROTHER, ERNST, 18 APRIL 1841

FIRSTLY, ALBERT ADDRESSED the issue of wastage. At Windsor Castle there was a centuries-old practice of feeding the poor, and as a result the castle kitchens produced far more food than was required by the household, whether the Queen and her family were in residence or not. The Master of the Household reported that in 1841 the castle had fed over 113,000 people, and Albert discovered that in one month alone over 800lb of Cheshire cheese had been consumed. He quickly put an end to this, and as there was always too much food prepared due to the '*à la française*' service style favoured at the Queen's table, which involved serving the dishes all at the same time, the Prince arranged for genuinely excess food to be donated to charity. Albert also suggested that the royal family cater for meals more frugally. During Christmas 1842 he convinced Victoria to order fewer dishes and less wine at dinner – to set a good example to the nation, he said. The Prince also restricted the number of candles allowed in visitors' rooms to two per day. Previously, extra candles had been sold by staff, who saw these opportunities as perks that went with the job. Albert's reforms were adhered to with stringency. When Madame Tietjens, the famous opera singer, arrived at Windsor in the 1850s she complained that the light in her quarters was too dim for her to prepare for her performance. The maid informed her that she could not have more than two candles, but she was allowed to cut the candles in half, to make four flames. Visitors also reported that matches were not provided in the bedrooms – guests were expected to take a lit candle up with them when returning at night.

TIMELINE OF
VICTORIAN INVENTIONS

OVER THE COURSE of Victoria's reign, domestic life was transformed by a series of inventions, many of which we take for granted today.

1840 ◈ Postage stamps

1841 ◈ Staplers

1843 ◈ Christmas cards

1845 ◈ Pneumatic tyres

1846 ◈ The sewing machine

1849 ◈ Safety pins

1852 ◈ The first public flushing toilet

1853 ◈ Post boxes

1855 ◈ Safety matches

1855 ◈ Rayon

1856 ◈ Pasteurisation

1858 ◈ Rotary washing machine

1860 ◈ Horse-drawn trams

1861 ◈ Yale locks

1863 ◈ The London Underground

1868 ◈ Traffic lights

1872 ◈ Mail-order catalogues

1873 ◈ The typewriter

1875 ◈ Chocolate Easter eggs

1876 ◈ The telephone

1876 ◈ The carpet sweeper

1878 ◈ Electric street lights

1878 ◈ Light bulbs

1880 ◈ Toilet paper

1883 ◈ The first electric railway

1884 ◈ The fountain pen

1885 ◈ The safety bicycle

1885 ◈ The petrol-powered motor car

1886 ◈ The dishwasher

1887 ◈ The gramophone

1888 ◈ Kodak box camera

1891 ◈ Escalators

1893 ◈ Zips

1894 ◈ Moving pictures

1895 ◈ X-rays

1896 ◈ Radio

1899 ◈ The motor-driven vacuum cleaner

Opposite clockwise from top left: Bryant & May's special safety match matchbox. An 1877 article about Alexander Graham Bell and the telephone. A George Jennings patented lavatory. One of Charles Babbage's calculating engines.

PORTION OF BABBAGE'S DIFFERENCE ENGINE.

ALBERT: Everyone deserves a second chance, Skerrett.

ALBERT ALSO CEASED the outdated practice of providing 'Red Room wine', which cost thirty-five shillings a week. The Red Room was set aside for officers and guards of the long-dead King George III, Victoria's grandfather, and the wine was supposed to be for their benefit. With the guardsmen no longer in situ, the junior staff had been utilising their allowance, which had never been cancelled. The staff at the royal palaces, of course, bitterly resented Albert's changes – especially the removal of toilet soap for their use and the fact that he stopped the option of tea instead of cocoa in the staff dining hall. These were small changes, but many of the servants had been in royal service for generations and looked on these practices as part and parcel of their entitlement. Royal wages were not generous, as evidenced by the huge salary increase the royal cook Francatelli enjoyed when he left the palace – it quadrupled. Albert, however, continued to make cuts, and the grumblings from below stairs grew louder – the Prince was behaving in a very high-handed manner.

'What a farce!'

~NEWSPAPER COMMENT ON ALBERT'S SINECURES

It was the cause of much resentment that Albert was himself in receipt of several 'sinecures' – highly paid positions conferred on him by Victoria to make up the shortfall in Parliament's allowance. Needless to say, Albert's war on waste did not extend to his own situation. Inevitably, a disgruntled servant ended up complaining to the press about the Prince's high-handed changes. Henry Saunders, Inspector of the Palace at Windsor, resigned his position and then spilled the beans and, as a result, journalist Henry Judge started to print parodies of the official Court Circular, based on the information he gleaned from Saunders. This was humiliating and made the Prince look like a bean counter. Albert took Judge to court and he won, but this did not make the Prince any more popular below stairs.

As well as turning his abilities to saving money, Albert also made money, increasing the revenues from the royal duchies. These were lands farmed for royal benefit in Cornwall and Lancaster. Revenue from the Duchy of Cornwall was passed to the infant Prince of Wales in 1841, and Albert did an astonishing job of managing the land on his son's behalf, almost quadrupling the duchy's income. Victoria was proud of her husband's progress and in August 1843 she invested £600 a year in the Duchy of Lancaster to improve the income from that as well. The public's curiosity was piqued, and rumours started to circulate that Albert was dabbling in railway shares, with cartoons and satirical articles in *Punch* magazine suggesting that this was where the new royal wealth was coming from.

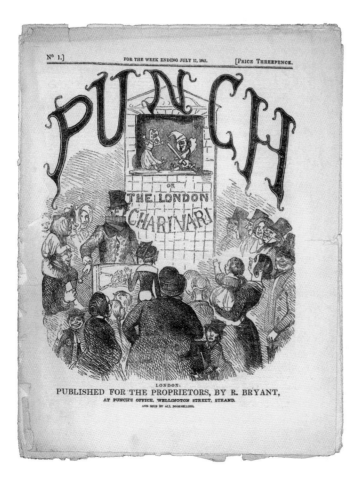

....
Left: The cover of the first issue of *Punch*.

SATIRE

SATIRE WAS A big part of Victorian culture. With no radio or television and high illiteracy rates, satirical cartoons, songs and theatrical performances were the way most people digested the news of the day. And for those who were more literate, pamphleteering was also a long-established British tradition. Pamphlets were circulated in public houses and included satirical poetry, poking fun at the Establishment.

Punch magazine, also known as *The London Charivari* (named after a Parisian magazine of the same name), was first published in July 1841. Under editor Mark Lemon and with founding capital of only £25 (around £1,000 in today's money – still not much to found a major publication), *Punch*'s first few years proved rocky, but over time the magazine became established as a stalwart of the publishing scene and employed several famous writers, illustrators and cartoonists. The word cartoon, as we understand it today, stems directly from early editions of the magazine. *Punch* was the highest quality of the satirical magazines, but there were many other more lowbrow publications in circulation, including the aptly named *Fun* magazine, which contained more risqué cartoons.

The money spent and demanded by the royals was a point satirists returned to again and again. When Victoria and Albert's engagement was announced, a popular poem did the rounds:

> *Quoth Hudibras of old 'a thing*
> *Is worth as much as it will bring.'*
> *How comes it then that Albert clear*
> *Has thirty thousand pounds a year?*

Satirists were also clear about who they thought was going to wear the britches in the forthcoming royal marriage:

> *She's all my Lehzen painted her,*
> *She's lovely and she's rich,*
> *But they tell me when I marry her*
> *That she will wear the britsch.*

Bawdy songs were also popular, particularly if they poked fun at the royal couple. The following song was published as a broadside and was sung to the tune of the National Anthem with a German accent in taverns and on stage:

> *God save sweet Vic, mine Queen*
> *Long live mine little Queen,*
> *God save de Queen*
> *Albert is victorious;*
> *De Coburgs now are glorious*
> *All so notorious, God Save the Queen*
>
> *Ah, Melbourne soon arise*
> *To get me de supplies –*
> *My means are small.*
> *Confound Peel's politics,*
> *Frustrate de Tory tricks,*
> *At dem now go like bricks,*
> *God damn dem all.*
>
> *The greatest gifts in store,*
> *On me be pleased to pour,*
> *And let me reign;*
> *Mine Vic has vowed today*
> *To honour and obey,*
> *And I will have de sway –*
> *Albert de King.*

Later, pamphleteers teased Victoria for her expensive tastes at the time when she was giving birth to the Princess Royal:

I must get all the things I can
A child's chair and a small brown pan,
Nine hundred and forty gallons of rum,
And a sponge to wash her little bum.

The royal couple were consistently portrayed as greedy and demanding of pomp and ceremony in these satirical works. And indeed, Victoria did often make the case for more public money to be allocated for her use, and the couple – particularly Albert – did stand on ceremony and demand a high level of respect from all visitors,

backing the allegations the satirists were making. One royal aide who worked with Albert for decades noted that he had never once been asked to sit in the Prince's presence. Albert was a stickler for such formalities – once, Victoria arranged to hide one of her heavily pregnant ladies from Albert's view at the opera so that the poor woman could sit down throughout the performance.

....

Below: A satirical cartoon of Queen Victoria as the landlady of a public house with Albert left holding the baby.

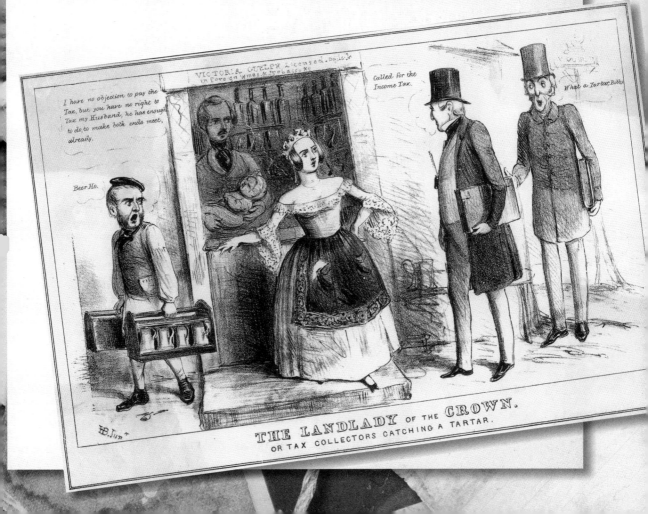

THE LANDLADY OF THE CROWN.
OR TAX COLLECTORS CATCHING A TARTAR.

10 February 1845

'Most parts of the palace are in a sad state and will ere long require further outlay to render them decent for the occupation of the Royal Family ... make use of this opportunity to remedy the exterior of the palace such as no longer to be a disgrace to the country which it certainly now is.'

LETTER FROM VICTORIA TO SIR ROBERT PEEL ON THE STATE OF BUCKINGHAM PALACE, 10 FEBRUARY 1845

WHEN VICTORIA WROTE to Sir Robert Peel in early 1845 complaining about the state of Buckingham Palace and asking for funds to renovate it, *Punch* ran a cartoon of the royal couple, cap in hand, with Albert addressing the poor of London. It was entitled 'A case of real distress'. In their favour, and unlike Victoria's Hanoverian forebears, the couple did contribute some funds for the changes they wanted to make by selling Brighton Pavilion, and as a result Peel gave way and Parliament granted matching funds for the renovations. Building work began on the palace, with a pavilion being erected in the grounds later that year and a new ballroom under construction.

SETS

'We built the whole set in nine weeks … We had all of the carpets printed and they were based on the real carpets at the palace. All of the chandeliers we had made in the Czech Republic, all of the furniture we had made in Malaysia … We gathered everything to create this world. We burned 12,000 candles while filming and used 3,500 square feet of gold leaf …'

MICHAEL HOWELLS, PRODUCTION DESIGNER, ON THE BUCKINGHAM PALACE SET

For series two of *Victoria*, more rooms were added to the set of Buckingham Palace, which was built in a huge aircraft hangar in the Yorkshire countryside. Just as Victoria and Albert did in real life, the production team extended the family space on set, adding a nursery, the Amber Drawing Room, music room and some servants' rooms. An extension to the throne room was also built. It's an enormous site, covering several thousand square feet, and quite disconcerting to walk from the open countryside into such detailed and unexpected splendour. Much of the set is built from wood and then painted or gilded – the flagstone floors are made in this way, as are the lavish marble fireplaces. The huge windows look out onto sections of

garden that are actually indoors and have been carefully constructed with huge lights hoisted on rigging to simulate daylight. The attention to detail is astonishing – a close examination is required to discover that the beautiful flower arrangements are not real – they are made of silk (some, by hand).

As well as the built interiors of Buckingham Palace, there are other locations that represent Victoria and Albert's main residence, including Bramham Park, Harewood House and Wentworth Woodhouse, where the exterior of the palace, including a twelve-foot-high wall and railings, has been constructed out of MDF covered in sand and painted to look like stone. The build took about a week. During the second series, there were times when two locations were both in use at once, stretching the tight twelve-person set team to the limit. You will often find shots from the built set and the real location appearing in the same scene – especially for kitchen scenes, where the real period kitchen

at Harewood House often features and the team has to shoot around the house's opening hours so the public can still have access.

Set designer Nick Wilkinson explains that 'controlling the period is the most difficult thing. You have to be eagle-eyed.' The team has to hide all switches and sockets and either remove or mask wires on the outside of buildings, as well as replacing modern windows and doors. They carefully take pictures of all the work they have done to ensure continuity.

On location, shooting can be disruptive for people and the team try to accommodate local businesses and residents alike. 'Flexibility is really important,' says Nick. The benefits of location shoots are manifold, though, as the results can be cunningly deceptive. While the scenes in Scotland were shot there, the scenes in France were actually filmed in Hartlepool, where a 'French quay' was set up with an old paddle boat representing the royal yacht *Victoria and Albert*. In real life, it wasn't seaworthy!

THE ROYAL COUPLE did not only have an eye on Buckingham Palace, however: Albert wanted to buy a holiday home. Brought up in the lush countryside of the Rosenau estate in Bavaria, he was keen to get his family out of the 'smoke-choked atmosphere of London'. Victoria wrote with some excitement in her diary that 'During our morning walk, Albert and I talked of building a place of our own.' As a start, Albert leased Osborne House on the Isle of Wight for the sum of £1,000 for the year. In 1845 he purchased the house and the surrounding countryside for £26,000, having beaten down the owners from the original asking price of £50,000.

Below: Osborne House, the couple's residence on the Isle of Wight.

OSBORNE HOUSE

SBORNE HOUSE ON the Isle of Wight was the first home Victoria and Albert chose together. Victoria wrote to her Uncle Leopold, on 25 March 1845, 'It is impossible to imagine a prettier spot,' and she reported that Albert had remarked that the view of the sea reminded him of the Bay of Naples. When they bought the estate later that year Victoria and Albert immediately set about demolishing the existing building and designing the home they really wanted – so at Osborne we see a true reflection of the royal couple's taste and style. The house was to be their home and it was designed around the needs of their young and growing family as well as those of court life.

Albert indulged his scientific interests and installed many innovations, including hot showers and baths and a cutting-edge ventilation system. Albert's passion for educating his children is also in evidence – he built a Swiss tree house, where the children learned to cook, installed a museum where they would study and built a mini-fort as a place where the young Princes could learn about military tactics. Victoria entertained extensively at this residence, but first and foremost the royal couple clearly considered it to be their home and many of the paintings and sculptures now on display there were the gifts they gave each other for birthdays and Christmas.

VICTORIA AND ALBERT were well matched in their attitude to financial affairs and, like her husband, the young Queen showed a fiscal rectitude that set her apart from her profligate uncles. When she came to the throne, before she fell in love with Albert, one of her first acts was to pay off her father's debts. Albert's reputation may have suffered as a result of his financial savvy, but Victoria's did not. The Prince was generally considered to be mean with money, and when the royal farms won prizes at agricultural shows it was considered particularly bad form that Albert pocketed the winnings and seemed happy to do so. His household reforms, however, meant that Victoria came to trust him, recognising his organisational skills, his clear thinking and the fact that he put his family first. While she had not complained about the old arrangements that had been overseen by Baroness Lehzen, she appreciated the new ones, especially as they afforded her a measure of financial independence from Parliament. She came to trust her husband absolutely as bit by bit he proved himself a shrewd manager.

The press of the day didn't realise that Albert also contributed to the finances of the Duchy of Saxe-Coburg and Gotha. The Prince maintained staff in Germany to look after his interests there and also invested in the local economy, including putting money into the early German railways. Had this fact hit the British newspapers, the matter would have been considered a national scandal. There was extreme sensitivity to the idea of British money being used to improve German estates. It was largely down to Albert, though, that Victoria's financial situation improved steadily over time; she may have come to the throne with a fairly generous allowance, but it was Albert – an accomplished and natural moderniser – who maximised her income.

Screenwriter Daisy Goodwin on writing *Victoria*...

THE SMELL OF THE PAST

The great joy of researching *Victoria* is that the legacy of her reign is everywhere. I live in a Victorian house. I eat from plates made to a Victorian design, sitting at a Victorian dining table. I write at a Victorian desk, although I draw the line at using a quill pen. Although I am writing about life nearly 180 years ago, I am constantly surprised by the similarities between then and now. We think that today is a time of instant communication, but a Victorian lady of letters would have thought nothing of sending a letter in the morning and getting a reply that same day. We think that spam email is a uniquely modern blight, but canny Victorian entrepreneurs used the telegraph in the same way, sending out blanket telegrams to householders to alert them to the merits of their upcoming sale of horsehair sofas and such like.

It was actually faster to travel from London to Dorset by train in the nineteenth century than it is now. The Victorians – the posh ones, anyway – had indoor plumbing, and by the end of the century electric light. Yes, the women wore disabling corsets that made slouching impossible, but how many women today wear shoes they can barely walk in? The technology and trappings are different, but the more I investigate, the more familiar the Victorian era feels. Except, of course, for the little matter of contraception. Having no control over your fertility must have made life

very difficult – I find it very hard to imagine the reality of having nine children, even with all the help that money can buy.

My favourite place to write is in the glorious Victorian confines of the London Library in St James's Square. This wonderful institution was founded in 1842 by the philosopher and historian Thomas Carlyle and was supported by Prince Albert himself. If you sit in the red leather armchairs in the reading room (where laptops are not allowed), it is quite easy to fancy yourself in the nineteenth century. The library has a unique collection of Victorian books and I have found wonderful gobbets in them that are ignored by modern biographers but are brilliant for a drama like *Victoria*. It was from a volume called *A Record of Royal Engagements* that I discovered that in the early years of their marriage Albert had fallen through the ice while skating on the lake in the gardens of Buckingham Palace and had to be rescued by Victoria. When I found this I was thrilled: it was just the set piece I needed for the Christmas episode – not only would it look spectacular, but it had the added advantage of pushing along the story for both characters. Albert is the sensible, thoughtful one in the marriage, but here he has to be rescued by Victoria, who is the only person light enough to crawl out onto the ice. He may dismiss her as a lightweight, but she has the strength when it counts.

Browsing through the magazines and newspapers that my characters would have read at the time (*Punch, The Illustrated London News, The Times, The Morning Chronicle*) is a great way of getting a sense of what was preoccupying people. I know what happens next, but my characters don't, so I always try to keep that idea of writing in the present.

It takes me about ten days to write an episode, but then there is a long and sometimes tortuous process of turning my script into something that is ready to be filmed. Unlike writing novels, when you are basically alone in a room, writing for TV is collaborative. I sometimes feel that a script is only finished when it is actually broadcast. It can be hard sometimes to keep your focus when there are so many different voices calling for masked balls or character arcs, but I have the great advantage of writing about a character who feels so real to me that when I say, 'Victoria wouldn't do that,' I feel that she would very much approve.

CHAPTER 7

THE
POWER
COUPLE

'Nobody who has paid any attention to the peculiar features of our present era will doubt for a moment that we are living at a period of most wonderful transition which tends rapidly to the accomplishment of that great end to which, indeed, all history points — the realisation of the unity of mankind.'

···· ALBERT TO THE FINE ART COMMISSION IN A SPEECH GIVEN AT THE MANSION HOUSE, 21 MARCH 1849 ····

VICTORIA AND ALBERT'S domestic situation was one thing, but the royal couple had a role to play in the wider world, and it turned out they were well-suited to it. Their first trip together further afield than England was when they set out for Scotland on 29 August 1842. When Victoria climbed aboard the *Royal George* at Woolwich, it was raining. As soon as the weather brightened, the Queen explored the yacht enthusiastically, even climbing a little way up the rigging to get a better view. 'How delightful to be quite alone together,' she enthused, by which she meant that the couple were only accompanied by servants, and had not brought their children or their entourage, which was travelling on a small flotilla of separate steamers further down the sound.

VISIT TO SCOTLAND

'The Queen cannot leave Scotland without a feeling of regret that her visit on the present occasion could not be further prolonged.'

LETTER FROM VICTORIA TO LORD ABERDEEN, 16 SEPTEMBER 1842

AT THE BEGINNING of September 1842, Victoria and Albert sailed into the Port of Leith at foggy Edinburgh. The Queen had been impatient to get to the Scottish capital, recording in her journal that the royal yacht simply hadn't gone fast enough. It had been a difficult year and the couple needed a break – Baroness Lehzen was leaving Buckingham Palace and one of the loyal governess's last duties was to look after the children while Victoria and Albert took this trip together. No royal monarch had visited Scotland in two decades – not since Victoria's uncle, George IV, had come to Edinburgh in 1822.

The couple spent a few days exploring the capital before heading out of town to Perthshire and on to the Highlands, where the hills, the heather and the lochs opened a new vista to the young Queen, who was still recovering from postnatal depression after the birth of her second child, Bertie, the year before. She sketched many of these views, and also locals in Highland dress, noting that the women were pretty and that, unlike in England, few wore any kind of hat or cap.

Albert often found their time visiting country estates rather boring, as he didn't enjoy country pursuits, but he appears to have enjoyed the trip regardless, perhaps because of Scotland's many forests, which may have reminded him of the forests in Coburg, of which he was particularly fond, and also

because he seems to have got on well with the Duke of Buccleuch, with whom they stayed at Dalkeith. Albert's relations with many English aristocrats were strained – they often viewed him as an interloper – but the Scottish lords did not have this attitude, or if they did, they hid it.

Victoria embraced the opportunity to relax. She took advantage of the light nights in the north and went pony riding in the hills as late as 11.30 p.m., which she declared 'the most romantic ride and walk I ever had'. The Queen was also enthusiastic about the bagpipe music at Lord Breadalbane's castle, where a round of nine pipers played her into meals. The couple read to each other, wrote and generally enjoyed themselves, flinging themselves into the round of formal dinners and Scottish country dancing, and spending some much-needed time alone. It was on this trip that Victoria first tried 'brose', or whisky and honey mixed together, which may have sparked her lifelong enjoyment of whisky. And knowing of the couple's fondness for dogs, the Duke of Buccleuch gave them a pair of Highland terriers when they left, which Victoria noted were 'very fine'.

Opposite: Queen Victoria and Prince Albert visiting Edinburgh, 3 September 1842 – the queen's first visit to Scotland.

VICTORIA'S LOVE OF Scotland meant that over time the country became increasingly considered an integral part of the United Kingdom, having previously been seen more as an outpost since the defeat of the final Jacobite uprising in 1746. She adored Scottish culture and Scottish writers, including Sir Walter Scott, and considered Scotland her personal retreat. This first visit in 1842 was an immediate success and within a decade Victoria and Albert would buy a home of their own in Scotland at Balmoral, which they furnished in the Highland style, using an abundance of tartan, stags' heads and thistle motifs.

ETIQUETTE

Historical advisor Alastair Bruce was on hand on set to help with royal and military etiquette during series two. 'We don't worry so much today because everything is more equal,' he says, 'but in the Victorian era everyone had a place and knew what to do. Communication was amazingly subtle.' Advising on the ins and outs from the early scriptwriting stage to the day the scenes were shot, Alastair is a key part of making sure that *Victoria* is historically accurate. His expertise is invaluable, particularly in scenes like the military parade shown in episode one where he advised on who takes a salute and who doesn't, where individual characters would have been placed and the sequence of ceremonial events.

'There is no doubt the team sought to bring the credibility of that time to the story. There are remarkable advantages to shaping the narrative to contrast with etiquette today,' he says. 'Life was more formal in every aspect.'

This is also true of scenes that take place in the personal sphere. Victoria and Albert were woman and man, wife and husband, but also queen and prince. 'There is a tension in that relationship,' Alastair comments. 'We tried to use deference, position and placing to allow the actors to play with it. Getting the protocol right really brought the story to life.'

VICTORIA:
Whatever happens,
we are united.
There are no secrets
between us.

THE VICTORIAN ERA was one of invention and innovation, and Victoria, encouraged by her young husband, became an early adopter of new technologies. In taking this attitude, the Queen and Prince supported British trade and popularised new ideas. Despite the criticism Albert received from the press for being penny pinching and foreign, and despite political issues such as Chartism causing popular unrest, the public was fascinated by the royal couple and they were still extremely influential. When Prince Albert wore a top hat for the first time in 1850, the old-style beaver and stovepipe hats soon faded from London's streets as everyone adopted this stylish new headgear. (He was notably a trendsetter rather than a follower – he refused, for example, to grow the elaborate facial hair sported by almost all Englishmen at the time.) Of course, such decisions were not always as arbitrary as merely sporting a particular hat or wearing your moustaches in a certain style – Victoria and Albert were well aware of the power they could confer on reliable tradespeople and modern advances, and they wanted to distribute that power wisely.

By way of a more formal endorsement, Victoria granted 'Royal Warrants' to trusted suppliers of goods to the Royal Household. This practice had been going on for decades, but the young Queen formalised it by setting up the Royal Warrant Holders Association in 1840. Carefully administered, warrant holders could display and advertise their royal patronage, and fashionable and upwardly mobile Britons flocked to emulate the taste of the royal couple. But Victoria and Albert went beyond simply recommending jam or soap powder, or influencing fashions. They also backed cutting-edge technological advances.

BEARDS

BEARDS WERE A male fashion vogue in Victorian Britain, particularly after the Crimean War. During previous eras men mostly went clean-shaven, but from early on in Victoria's reign there was a move towards the growing of elaborate beards. When soldiers returned from the Middle East and Africa sporting full beards, the trend fully took off and male facial hair became synonymous with heroism and bravery. In fact, many of the returning soldiers had grown beards because it had been impossible to get shaving soap and other supplies while they were on active military service. Prince Albert refused to conform to the fashion for large, bushy facial hair and continued to trim his whiskers. This may have been because Victoria wasn't keen on large beards or moustaches – later in her reign she even campaigned to have moustaches banned in the Navy.

Meanwhile, the British fashion craze for beards spread to America, popularised by illustrations in magazines. In 1844, Charles Dickens proclaimed of his own facial hair that 'the moustaches are glorious, glorious. I have cut them short, and trimmed them a little at the ends to improve their shape. They are charming, charming. Without them, life would be a blank.' Alfred, Lord Tennyson, Victoria's favourite poet, grew a beard much to the consternation of his wife, who objected at every turn. Tennyson did not remove it.

Bearded men became such a common sight that they were even given nicknames, such as 'Dundrearies', named after a character in a play, and 'Piccadilly weepers' after fashionable men about town who frequented the Piccadilly area of London's West End. Even styles were given particular names – the terms 'mutton chop whiskers', for example, and 'sideburns' were both coined in this period.

Facial hair became so strongly identified with masculinity that men who couldn't grow a beard sometimes resorted, in their shame, to quack lotions that claimed to 'cure' their beardlessness (few of which worked). In response to this new demand, a whole industry sprang up to produce artificial beards. Wig makers stocked different styles and colours in large quantities. The shelves of pharmacies and barbers were stocked with beard oils, waxes and specialised scissors to trim beard hair. Beard oil was known as Macassar oil, after the Indonesian port where it was said to originate. Men used so much of it that 'antimacassars' came into fashion – doilies that were placed on soft furnishings to protect the upholstery from the oil. Advice and discussion around beards was printed in pamphlets and newspapers. Several books were written on the subject and sold well, including *The Gentleman's Book of Etiquette*, which offered various advice on looking after the reader's beard at home – 'a steady hand', apparently, is what was required.

....

Opposite: Late Victorian advertisement for Pears' Soap.

ALBERT:
So you prefer to ignore scientific progress in favour of tradition?

VICTORIA:
I prefer tried-and-tested ideas to newfangled notions, yes.

ALBERT'S SCIENTIFIC EDUCATION was key to deciding which innovations were chosen for support and which weren't. After he married Victoria he proved himself a dedicated family man, but from the start he was also keen to carve out a larger role in public life. Albert loved 'improvements' and, as he had proved within the Royal Household, he had a keen organisational mind. Early in the marriage, between 1843 and 1844, the Prince turned his hand to redesigning the British military helmet, which he based on a design already in use in Germany. Albert's idea was not initially popular because it was 'foreign' and many believed that the showier feathered red helmets already in use were important as a mark of British status and military glory, but the Prince's green helmet was more practical and less of a target on the battlefield. The shape he came up with is known as the Prince Albert pattern and was, in time, adopted by several regiments. Albert loved uniforms and discussed military caps with Napoleon III when the two men met in 1854.

The Prince Consort was also fascinated by photography, and the portrait taken of him by William Constable in Brighton in 1842 is one of the earliest photographic portraits in the world. Victoria and Albert's patronage launched this new technology and promoted it as an art form as well as a science. The royal couple attended exhibitions, became patrons of the newly formed Photographic Society of London and generously commissioned portraits of family members as well as public events, ensuring that this new medium was immediately given a high public profile. As a result, both industry and the upper classes flocked to adopt this new technology, and from this royal beginning it expanded into wider society.

Likewise the young couple enjoyed the burgeoning railways – Victoria took great delight in the speed at which she could now travel between residences. 'I am quite charmed by it,' she wrote to her uncle Leopold on 14 June 1842, and once the Queen had chosen to travel by train, soon everyone wanted to do the same. While Victoria and Albert gave their approval to their chosen causes willingly, they also expected their support to be appreciated. The Queen was horrified, for example, after opening Newcastle Station in 1850, to be presented with a bill for the banquet and festivities she had attended. Thereafter she always had the blinds lowered when she went through Newcastle Station. She also had her carriage blinds lowered when she travelled through the Midlands, as she felt the Industrial Revolution had blighted the landscape and the view of the factories distressed her.

VICTORIA:
I am sure he will appreciate your help with the Sanitation Commission, Uncle, while I attend to affairs of state. I don't spend all my time in the nursery.

PRINCE ALBERT'S STUDIO.

Left: An illustration from Punch of Albert as the designer of the military helmet.

THE RAILWAYS

When Victoria came to the throne, the first public railways had already been built, but they were local rail links operated by small companies. Over the first decade of her reign, however, almost the entire UK network was laid down, meaning the vast majority of towns and villages now had a rail connection. Railways were an improvement on canal transport (they didn't freeze in winter) and were quicker and more reliable for long-distance travel than road or sea.

A bubble of investment speculation known as 'railway mania' came to a peak in 1846, and although some companies failed, as investors sank their savings into badly thought-out schemes, others thrived. By the end of the decade the British railway system was in good order and the impact it had on the day-to-day lives of the British population was legion. The railways became a major employer. Factories sprang up along the railway lines and the coal, iron and steel industries benefited from the boom. The postal service took advantage of this quick, easy and cheap method of transporting mail, and immediately it became possible for daily newspapers to be circulated nationally. Farming and fishing communities suddenly found they could transport their goods to market without fear of foodstuffs spoiling, while towns along the routes grew and some local brands became national players almost overnight – including Rowntree's, Cadbury and Guinness. And crucially, people could live further away from where they worked, and

so middle-class suburban life blossomed as builders bought plots to develop good-quality housing along the railway routes.

Victoria took her first train journey from Slough to Paddington on 13 June 1842. There were sixteen royal carriages available to Victoria and Albert as each railway company vied with the others to design the most tempting compartments to lure the royal couple aboard their train, so the Great Western Railway Company were ecstatic when the Queen chose their carriage to make her first public trip. *The Times* said of the luxurious royal saloon that 'the fittings are upon a most elegant and magnificent scale, tastefully improved by bouquets of rare flowers arranged within the carriage'. Driven by Isambard Kingdom Brunel, the famous engineer, Victoria's first trip took 25 minutes for the 18-mile journey. The following day *The Times* reported: 'Yesterday Her Majesty the Queen … returned from her sojourn at Windsor Castle, accompanied by … Prince Albert … The intention of Her Majesty to return to town by railroad … [was] carried into effect with the greatest secrecy.'

Though she enjoyed the trip, Victoria became nervous when the engine went full pelt and afterwards she issued orders limiting trains to 30mph in the dark and 40mph in daylight if she was on board. The Great Western Railway subsequently fitted a signal to the roof of the royal saloon so the royal party could signal to the train's driver to slow down if necessary. Victoria also refused to dine in her carriage

and insisted on stopping every two hours to use the lavatory. In fact, she never got used to interconnecting carriages and simply stopped the train when she wanted to go from one carriage to another.

It was after Victoria's trip that rail travel really blossomed. The royal seal of approval can only have helped build confidence in this new mode of transport as one that was suitable for people of quality. The railways had truly arrived.

....

Above: Queen Victoria and the royal family boarding the train for Scotland.

ADA LOVELACE:
As a woman who prefers numbers to needlework, I have always been an anomaly.

VICTORIA'S LIFE STOOD in sharp contrast to those of most women (even the privileged ones) of her era, who enjoyed no legal status and few rights. Victorian society spawned many unusual women – explorers like Isabella Bird, medical pioneers such as Elizabeth Garrett Anderson and scientists like Ada Lovelace (see also pages 214–15) – but none had the power and rights that Victoria enjoyed. She wasn't an equal partner in her marriage to Albert, she was the boss – and both he and the wider world knew it. Every time a British citizen used the new 'Penny Post' Royal Mail service, the Queen's profile was affixed to the envelope, drawing the association with Her Majesty whenever a missive was dispatched. Victoria was an icon and she insisted on keeping royal political power in her own hands. This meant that, initially in their marriage, Albert was forced to find ways to contribute that weren't merely political. Though the couple fought often about this issue, the Prince did find solutions and his scientific interests proved a fruitful early outlet for his talents.

By the time Samuel F. B. Morse electrically transmitted his famous message, 'What hath God wrought?' from Washington to Baltimore on 24 May 1844, the Prince had already heard of this exciting new form of communication – the telegraph. He insisted on having a demonstration, immediately realised its potential and had a telegraph office installed at Buckingham Palace so the royal couple could send and receive news. It wasn't long before the telegraph became closely associated with the railways; telegraph lines were laid initially between Euston and Camden stations in London and then rapidly across the whole rail network as it grew. In 1850 (years after Albert's telegraph office had been established), the first cable was laid under the English Channel so that news became instantly available internationally. These innovations made Buckingham Palace one of the most exciting and well-connected residences in the world. Albert was indeed a visionary in being able to spot these key advances and back them when it mattered.

ADA LOVELACE

'The best and wisest refuge from all troubles is in . . .science.'
ADA LOVELACE

ADA LOVELACE WAS the only legitimate child of the Romantic poet Lord Byron and his wife, Anne Isabella Milbanke. Byron, the aristocratic wild child of his generation, left the country pursued by scandal just months after Ada was born, and she was brought up by her mother's family. Byron died in Greece when Ada was only eight years of age. As a little girl, she was watched constantly in case she had inherited her father's wild nature, which her mother considered a form of madness. She wasn't allowed to see a portrait of Byron until she was twenty years old.

'I am ... the bride of science.'
ADA LOVELACE

Ada developed scientific interests from a young age. As a teenager, recovering from a bout of measles, she drew up a detailed scientific plan of the equipment she would need to be able to fly. She called this her theory of 'flyology'. Ada was tutored in mathematics by noted researcher and author Mary Somerville, and as an adult she worked with Charles Babbage on his pioneering machines, the 'difference engine' and the 'analytical engine', the forerunners of today's computers. Babbage called her the 'enchantress of numbers'. During the course of her work with Babbage, Ada wrote what is considered by many to be the world's first computer program. She also carried out electrical experiments and towards the end of her life was rumoured to be working on a project that related mathematics to music.

Ada was presented at court at the age of seventeen and a few years later, in 1835, she married William, 8th Baron King and 1st Earl of Lovelace, and had three children with him. Ten years older than her, Ada's husband was broadly supportive of her work, though despite her pioneering studies Ada was dogged by financial worries due to her gambling habits. She was not interested in fashion, and was once unflatteringly described as being 'not so well dressed as her maid'.

She died young in 1852 at the age of thirty-six. A blue plaque is raised to commemorate Lady Lovelace in St James's Square, London, and several scientific awards and prizes are named in her memory. She has also appeared as a fictional character in several plays and novels. Ada is buried next to Lord Byron, the father she never knew, at the Church of St Mary Magdalene in Hucknall, Nottinghamshire.

....

Opposite: Portraits of Ada Lovelace.

ALBERT:
It is magnificent.
Sir Robert has
asked me to be the
Patron of the
new Parliament
building.

THE PRINCE ALSO turned his attention to transforming the landscape around him. Apart from the domestic changes he instigated at Buckingham Palace and other royal residences, he was also appointed to the committee charged with rebuilding the Palace of Westminster – the British Parliament buildings in London. The original building had been destroyed by fire in 1834; thousands of Londoners had watched in awe as the building burned and the famous painter J. M. W. Turner later depicted the scene from memory. Work on the new parliament building was already underway when Victoria married Albert, and a public competition to design it had been won by the architect Charles Barry, who brought a talented younger man, Augustus Pugin, onto his team. Pugin is now widely credited with the iconic design of the main body of the Houses of Parliament, and particularly the interiors.

'Now there is one thing to be lamented in this country. Our nobility are ignorant of the art of sculpture. In my country at the university when I learnt Greek, I was taught principles of Greek art, for one illustrates the other.'

~ALBERT TALKING ABOUT HIS ROLE IN DESIGNING
THE NEW HOUSE OF COMMONS IN CONVERSATION
WITH SCULPTOR JOHN GIBSON AT OSBORNE HOUSE

Albert took on the role of chairing the commission to advise the government on the rebuilding and quickly set up a Fine Arts Commission, charged with choosing paintings and other artefacts to decorate the new building. This was one of the most important patronage jobs of the age and Albert immediately sought advice from his former tutors in Germany, causing an outcry yet again about 'foreign influence'. So the Prince cleverly set up several exhibitions to fire public interest in the project. It was said that between 20,000 and 30,000 people visited the exhibitions each day while they were open in London. 'All England went to see it. All the omnibuses were covered with placards advertising it,' one contemporary gushed.

Albert then personally oversaw the making of the artworks chosen, working closely with the artists and on one occasion making hands-on changes to a statue of his wife, which was being modelled by the famous sculptor, John Gibson.

But Albert wasn't only interested in the hallowed halls of Westminster. The attention to detail that fired his huge enthusiasm impacted scientific and artistic projects nationwide, and although Victoria and Albert didn't actually open the Thames Tunnel, as depicted in the series, these kinds of projects were top of Albert's lists of interests.

SIR ROBERT PEEL:
The Prince takes
a keen interest in
the arts, Duchess.

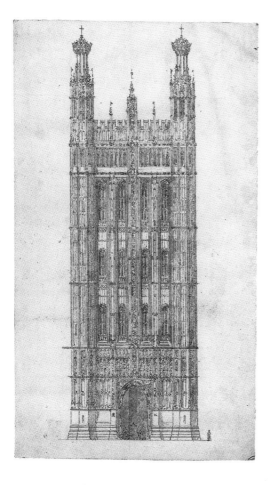

Left: Drawing for the Houses of Parliament, 1836–40.

THE THAMES TUNNEL

THE THAMES TUNNEL was a visionary project – the first tunnel in the world to run under a navigable river. The tunnel ran from Rotherhithe to Wapping and took almost twenty years to build, cost several lives due to disastrous and unexpected flooding and was the subject of wry satirical verse across the capital – would the great engineer Isambard Kingdom Brunel's grand project ever be completed? It had to be refinanced more than once, running well over budget.

> Good Monsieur Brunel
> Let misanthropy tell
> That your work, half complete, is begun ill;
> Heed them not, bore away
> Through gravel and clay,
> Nor doubt the success of your Tunnel.

> That very mishap,
> When the Thames forced a gap,
> And made it fit haunt for an otter,
> Has proved that your scheme
> Is no catchpenny dream; –
> They can't say "twill never hold water.'

....

Opposite: Brunel's pioneering work Thames Tunnel.

When the tunnel finally opened in 1843, it was dubbed the eighth wonder of the world – 'a shining avenue of light to Wapping'. On its first day it is estimated that 50,000 people paid a penny each to walk its length, understandably taking huge delight in strolling underneath the water of the River Thames. Over the first month almost a million people visited the attraction. Though it was designed to take carriages, the tunnel never opened to traffic and was initially used solely by pedestrians. In 1852 a huge 'Fancy Fair' was thrown underground and proved a great draw to the crowds, but in 1869 the Thames Tunnel was closed to the public and taken over by the railway.

That said, it was a huge achievement. Before the tunnel, it took a cargo ship as long to cross the Thames as it did to reach New York.

Though the tunnel was a feat of engineering, and despite the initial huge visitor numbers, it was a financial disaster. It never carried cargo as intended – the sheer number of ships travelling up and down the Thames every day meant that getting cargo across the river was problematic, and the tunnel could have provided a quicker and cheaper crossing, had it been utilised. The project, however, did prove an inspiration for others across the UK, including the Severn Tunnel and Mersey Railway Tunnel, which greatly benefited from the lessons learned by Brunel and his team in their pioneering work.

Der Tunnel.

WILHELMINA:
I have heard that when
Mr Brunel ran out of
money he held a dinner
underwater for investors.

THE THAMES TUNNEL.

ALBERT:
Some new music
came today.
Schubert. We should
play together.
That might cure you
of this strange
mood, *Liebes*.

THE PRESSING SOCIAL issues of the day also galvanised the Prince into action. In 1846, shocked by the poverty he had witnessed on his rides outside the palace walls, Albert became president of the Society for Improving the Condition of the Labouring Classes. This was something the Queen herself could not have done as it would have been considered inappropriate, but his work to provide affordable housing was desperately needed and the Prince's example encouraged the upper and middle classes to take responsibility for the poverty around them, at the same time as creating a template for royal benevolence. Albert is said to have promised that he would 'never stop promoting [this cause] wherever and whenever I can'. In 1847 he also became chancellor of the University of Cambridge and set about modernising the antiquated system of teaching, instigating new courses, particularly in the sciences, which made Cambridge one of the most cutting-edge places to study in Europe. Robert Rhodes James, the Conservative politician, said Albert was responsible for a 'spectacular revival of Cambridge University from medieval slumber to a world eminence it has never surrendered'.

Meanwhile, at home and about town the royal couple became cultural patrons. Victoria enjoyed the theatre and she and Albert attended often, as well as having several productions staged at the palace. They were great supporters of the arts, encouraging everything from high art to more novelty forms of entertainment. While they would watch celebrated actors in Shakespearean plays like *Othello*, they would also enjoy the occasional lion tamer. In 1837 Victoria insisted on returning six times in six weeks to watch the famous American lion tamer Isaac van Amburgh risk his life in a cage of big cats in his show on Drury Lane. And when Amburgh returned to London in the 1840s, Victoria took Albert with her to see him yet again. The Prince, for his part, was fond of music and early in Victoria's reign a biannual State Concert became a regular feature of the royal programme. Victoria's Maids of Honour were expected to sing and be able to play the piano and sight-read sheet music.

Albert expanded the Queen's 'Private Band' into a full orchestra and insisted that the musicians not only play background music for royal dinners but also concerts at the royal palaces. The first royal knighthoods to musicians were given during Victoria's reign – twenty in all, starting in 1842 with Henry Bishop, who wrote 'Home, Sweet Home'. Victoria loved dancing (she especially loved the ballet) and the royal couple regularly put on balls, sometimes coming up against severe opposition, as with the Plantagenet Ball featured in the series. The Queen particularly enjoyed 'God Save the Queen' played as a polka.

IRA ALDRIDGE

IRA ALDRIDGE WAS an American
entertainer who took the European theatre
world by storm during Victoria's reign. As the
first black man to play major Shakespearean
roles in Britain, he was also a pioneer. Born
in New York in 1807, he arrived in England at
the age of eighteen and made his London stage
debut in October 1825. He was known as the
'African Roscius' – named after a famous actor
in Ancient Rome – and became known for his
starring roles as Othello, King Lear, Shylock,
Macbeth and Hamlet (when Aldridge played
traditionally white characters, he used
greasepaint and a wig). Edmund Kean – a
superstar of the London stage – praised Aldridge's
'wonderful versatility' early on in his career.

In April 1833, having played at the Theatre
Royal in Dublin and the Theatre Royal in Bath,
and having managed the Coventry Theatre for a
while, he returned to London to play Othello at
the Theatre Royal in Covent Garden, only to be
met with an outcry in the popular press about
a black actor being given a leading role and a
campaign to 'drive him from the stage'. It did not
succeed, however, and after the performance even
his critics couldn't help admitting that Aldridge
had huge talent. Many newspapers carried
glowing reviews. The *Standard* called him a
'singularly gifted actor' and the *Spectator* said he
'evinced a great deal of feeling and nature in his
performance'. Aldridge became hugely famous,
though the controversy of casting a black actor
followed him throughout his career.

In 1825 he married an Englishwoman,
Margaret Gill, and together they had a son, who
later emigrated to Australia. In 1852 Aldridge left
the UK and toured Europe, where he was
presented at several royal courts, knighted in
Germany and banned in Russia, where the Tsar

took exception to the story of *Macbeth* because
the play is essentially about murdering a king.

When Gill died after forty years of marriage,
Aldridge married a self-styled Swedish countess
– Amanda von Brandt. They had four children,
three of whom went on to have starring roles
on the stage, particularly in opera.

Prejudice in the wider community was rife,
fired by 'scientific' theories, which held that
whites were the superior race. James Hunt,
President of the London Anthropological
Society, wrote in his paper 'The Negro's place in
nature' that 'the Negro is inferior intellectually
to the European ...' While Hunt's comments
went against the general tide of opinion and
were greeted with boos and hisses (mostly
because he was advocating slavery) public
sentiment was mixed. Aldridge must have felt
most at home in Britain, though, because in
1863, at the age of fifty-six, he became a
British subject.

Sadly, only four years later he died on tour
in Poland. There are several theatre companies
named after him and they continue to
champion black acting talent, in both Britain
and the United States. A bronze plaque was
raised to his memory – the only one to a black
actor – at the Shakespeare Memorial Theatre in
Stratford-upon-Avon. Despite the initial
animosity he met with, Aldridge clearly trusted
British audiences and once wrote that he 'might
have feared that, unknown and unfriended, he
had little claim to public notice' but that 'being
a foreigner and a stranger are universal passports
to British sympathy'.

....

Opposite top: Ira Aldridge playing the part of Aaron in
Shakespeare's *Titus Andronicus* on stage. Opposite below:
Aldridge in theatrical costume.

my dear Brother you must do what you
Galway March 7 1807
Guinness Mahon & Co

THE PLANTAGENET BALL

N 12 MAY 1842 the Queen held the magnificent, invitation-only Plantagenet Ball at Buckingham Palace. It was held to support the work of the Spitalfields silk weavers. The ball was fancy dress and all of high society was invited. With the finances of the country in dire straits, however, Victoria's decision had been the subject of some controversy. It was not a good time to splash money on a showcase event – riots had taken place in the Midlands and the North, fired by the hunger of the poor and frustration that the pioneering Chartist movement was making little headway in its aims to democratise British society. Factory wages had recently dropped by 25 per cent and many ordinary families were not able to cover the basic costs of living. When Victoria insisted that the ball would stimulate trade and continued with her plans regardless, she came in for public criticism. *Punch* satirised the ball by contrasting the 'purple dress' of the revelling rich with the 'cerecloth' or shrouds worn by the destitute. Another newspaper printed a list of the names of people said to have recently starved to death in England alongside the ball's expenses.

An estimated 18,000 people were employed in readying the palace and the guests for the occasion, with a great deal of attention paid to detail. It is said that the expert dramatist James Robinson Planché, who helped to design both Victoria and Albert's costumes for the party, was inundated with requests from guests seeking advice about what to wear, and that seamstresses within miles of London worked into the night to ready the fabulous costumes that had been ordered. Victoria took a keen interest in both her own costume and Albert's, sketching them herself for her seamstresses to work from. The Prince was dressed as King Edward III – it was a chance for Albert to wear a crown – (although it was noted that he did not trim his whiskers), and his costume was edged with 1,200 hand-sewn pearls. Victoria dressed as Edward's queen, Philippa. Her lavish silk dress was made entirely in London at Spitalfields, and her upper abdomen was covered by a diamond stomacher valued at the time at £60,000 – around £2.5 million in today's money.

Victoria and Albert anxiously inspected the palace before the guests arrived and Victoria declared the Throne Room 'really quite beautiful, the alcove & throne, all hung with dark blue cloth with gold crown & Garter printed all over the hangings'. When over 2,000 guests flooded into Buckingham Palace that night, the Queen was delighted to see that a huge effort had gone into their costumes. Many men had hired full suits of armour. Dancing ensued – Victoria records enjoying the quadrilles and mazurkas – and the party went on until three in the morning.

The Plantagenet Ball was such a huge social success that Victoria and Albert commissioned a new ballroom at Buckingham Palace at a cost of £45,000, including central heating, built-in gas lighting and easy proximity to the upgraded kitchens below. The room was declared one of the most beautiful for dancing in England and ran to 123 feet long and 60 feet wide.

The silk workers at Spitalfields, whom Victoria had wanted to support, did receive a good deal of work as a result of the publicity the ball afforded their silks, and the charities set up to support the Spitalfields community also had a flood of contributions. However, the outcry continued that the ball was a waste of money and many argued that if the huge sum spent on the ball had been given directly to those in need, more good might have been done.

Victoria was unrepentant. The royal couple's beautiful outfits were commemorated in a double portrait by Edwin Landseer, commissioned by the Queen the following year, 1843. National newspapers also commissioned their own engravings of the guests in their fabulous costumes, and many of those who attended had drawings and lithographs made of them in their fancy-dress finery, so that a good record still exists of what the assembled guests wore on this most glamorous and controversial night at Buckingham Palace.

....

Below: Victoria and Albert in costume at the Plantagenet Ball.

ALBERT STILL FELT frustrated by his role, and he and Victoria continued to argue over the years, wrestling over control of what was and wasn't suitable territory for a queen on the one hand and her prince consort on the other. However, publicly, together, they changed the face of Britain. By sheer vigour and force of interest, the young couple won over the early critics who felt that Victoria was too young and inexperienced or that Albert was too foreign. Slowly, but surely, they became well regarded for their pioneering attitude and hard work, as well as for their social and cultural contribution to public life.

It's unlikely that any other constitutional monarch ever had as much influence on the day-to-day lives of their subjects as Victoria did, and without Albert it would have been impossible. 'For what has not my beloved and perfect Albert done? Raised monarchy to the highest pinnacle of respect, and rendered it popular beyond what it *ever* was in this country,' Victoria enthused in a letter to her Uncle Leopold in 1858. She herself remains remarkably visible in public life today, and although only 15 per cent of the statues in the UK are raised to women, most of them are dedicated to her.

CHAPTER 8

THE FACE OF AN EMPIRE

'Affairs go on, and all will take some shape or other, but it keeps one in hot water all the time.'

···· LETTER FROM VICTORIA TO LEOPOLD,
KING OF THE BELGIANS, 15 JUNE 1841 ····

VICTORIA AND ALBERT were domestic figureheads for the nation but also international figureheads for the British Empire, which grew immensely during the course of the Queen's reign. But in an era before photography, Victoria often went unrecognised when on her travels. In 1843, when she first visited the King of France, Louis-Philippe I, she was strolling on the deck of the royal yacht *Victoria and Albert* in her black travelling gown and bonnet when she was handed a parcel by a Frenchwoman. 'Take this, they are cakes for the Queen. Take care of them. Now mind, don't fail to give them her,' the bemused Queen was told. On another occasion she was greeted by the elderly Lord Portarlington with 'I know your face quite well, but I cannot put a name to it.' Victoria took these episodes in good humour – given the pressures of the job, it might even have been a relief for this lively young girl to feel like an ordinary person once in a while.

HMY *VICTORIA AND ALBERT*

HMY *VICTORIA AND ALBERT* was a twin-paddle steamer launched on 25 April 1843, built at Pembroke Dock in West Wales and designed by naval reformer Sir William Symonds. It was owned and operated by the Royal Navy and kept exclusively for royal use, replacing the HMY *Royal George*, which was decommissioned. *Victoria and Albert* weighed 1,034 tons, carried two guns and was the first royal yacht to be steam powered – it was fitted with a huge 430-horsepower engine.

Victoria and Albert used the yacht for their trip to Le Tréport, France, in 1843. Victoria recorded in her diary that she woke early, 'there being nothing as proper curtains to keep out the light' in her cabin. However, the couple enjoyed the small yacht and took it out over twenty times during its lifetime, mainly staying in British coastal waters around the south coast of England.

ALBERT UNDERSTOOD THAT entertainment was vital to keep his young wife happy, so while childbearing took its toll on Victoria, he dedicated himself to looking after the Queen, organising holidays to get her out of London. It was good for Victoria to take these breaks from her duties and enjoy some private time, but she couldn't stay away for long. London was the flagship of all things British, and back at home in Buckingham Palace she and Albert set about establishing themselves – both determined to work hard and do their best in the business of representing the country, not only at home, but on the world stage, too.

The reality was that, internationally, Britain's fortunes were on the wane in the 1840s. George III, Victoria's grandfather, had 'lost' the thirteen American colonies in 1776 during the American War of Independence and, taking over from Lord Melbourne, Prime Minister Sir Robert Peel was presiding over a straitened economic policy. Britain was poor and Victoria herself was not as wealthy as many of her aristocratic counterparts. There were genuine concerns about handing over huge amounts of public money to royalty while the country's economy was failing and the majority of British people were living in filthy, grinding poverty.

ALBERT:
Liebes, it is too soon after your confinement.

Opposite: Queen Victoria and Prince Albert arriving at the Royal Dockyard on HMY *Victoria and Albert*, Woolwich, 1843.

VICTORIAN POVERTY

'Two nations between whom there is no intercourse and no sympathy; who are ignorant of each other's habits, thoughts and feelings ... fed by different food ... ordered by different manners and not governed by the same laws. The Rich and the Poor.'

POLITICIAN BENJAMIN DISRAELI IN HIS NOVEL *SYBIL*, DESCRIBING ENGLAND, 1845

FOR MANY RICH people in the Victorian era, the only time they came into protracted contact with the poor was on the pages of Charles Dickens's novels. Poverty was considered by many to be a 'natural condition' of anybody who worked with their hands. As improvements were made to farming yields through new methods and machinery, the working class moved in a wave from the countryside to the town, where often there simply wasn't enough work for them, especially if they didn't have a trade.

The term 'working class' did not always mean a person was poor; class could be quite distinct from earnings. A coachmaker in London, for example, would be considered working class, but earned five pounds and five shillings a week, as his skills were in demand. This was considerably more than many middle-class clerks might bring home. At the bottom of the working-class barrel were the labourers, who earned only twenty to thirty shillings a week – an amount on which it would have been difficult to meet the most basic needs. There was very little employment legislation at the beginning of Victoria's reign, and the working poor had to put in unspeakable hours.

In London, those in need did their best. 'Mudlarks' waded into the filthy waters of the Thames to retrieve anything they might sell. Boys might hold a horse's reins for a gentleman or collect dog pooh for sale in the tannery industry. Some earned a meagre living sweeping the filthy streets to clear a path for rich pedestrians. Begging was illegal but that didn't stop it going on, with many men, women and children simply asking for money on the streets, especially if they had an obvious disability.

Many of the poor were willing to work but they were dependent on jobs being available. The docks in London, for example, kept few standing staff and simply took on men at a low rate of pay as they needed them. Crowds would form at the gates of the yard each morning in the hope that a big order had come in. If the weather was bad the men and their families would simply not have a wage coming in that week. Women who worked in factories or sweatshops were in a similar situation; if there were no orders, there was no pay.

If their situation became truly unbearable, the poor could admit themselves to the workhouse. This was the only comprehensive public help available, and it was seen as a way of controlling the poor and keeping them off the streets. For the poor it was a last resort, as families were split up on entry to the house, the work was backbreaking, the food dreadful and the conditions hard.

Unsurprisingly, this grim state of affairs took its toll and death rates for the poor were extraordinarily high. There was hardly any medical care available and most suffered from malnutrition, so if they became ill they stood a much lower chance of survival than their well-fed social superiors.

....

Opposite right: Mudlarks scouting in the Thames for things to sell.
Opposite left: Punch cartoon, 1843.

PUNCH'S PENCILLINGS.—No. LXII.

" OF POOR-LAW " KINDNESS."

THE CHEF AT Buckingham Palace, Charles Elmé Francatelli, had a strong social conscience and helped to set up soup kitchens. He declared he 'could feed every day a thousand families on the food that was wasted in London' and wrote *A Plain Cookery Book for the Working Classes*, which was published in 1852 and included cheap recipes using offal and foraged food.

LOUIS PHILIPPE:
What do you say in
English, the iron fist
in the velvet glove?
You look so *mignonne*
and yet underneath
you are Boadicea!

VICTORIA AND ALBERT were determined to work together to build a vision of the monarchy that not only represented the country, but also promoted it abroad. They had a lot to prove. At the start of Victoria's reign, France was seen as the major imperial power in the world, and it was also Britain's main enemy. Victoria and Albert's 1843 trip to visit the King of France (who had been a close friend of Victoria's father) marked the Queen's first royal visit overseas. Victoria relished her time in France and as she was welcomed for the first time on foreign soil she declared that 'the cheering of the people, and of the troops, crying "*Vive la Reine! Vive le Roi!*" – well nigh overcame me.'

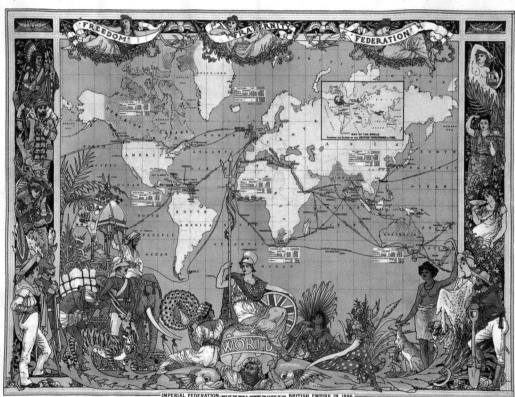

Above: Map of the British Empire during the 1800s.

VICTORIA & ALBERT'S
VISIT TO FRANCE

1 SEPTEMBER 1843
Left Plymouth on HMY *Victoria and Albert*,
passing Falmouth and Pendennis

2 SEPTEMBER 1843
Passed by Cherbourg, greeted at the rock
known as the Pluton, passed Dieppe and went
on to Eu, where they were greeted by the King's
Barge and taken to the château at Le Tréport

3 SEPTEMBER 1843
At the château – riding, etc.

4 SEPTEMBER 1843
At St Pierre en Valle along the Route
Clementine

5 SEPTEMBER 1843
At Le Tréport

6 SEPTEMBER 1843
Picnic in the forest at St Catherine

7 SEPTEMBER 1843
Sailed back to Brighton on the HMY
Victoria and Albert to meet with their
children at the Pavilion

Top right: Queen Victoria and Prince Albert on the visit to Paris, 1843.

MAKE-UP

'The make-up was obviously very minimal; it was mostly trying to make everyone feel comfortable in their skin on set. The challenges for the team were to create that many hairstyles and different looks.'

NIC COLLINS, MAKE-UP DESIGNER

Make-up had been common at court during previous eras, but in Victoria's day it was associated with 'show' girls and prostitutes, and respectable women did not wear any (though some privileged women cheated and wore a light dusting of rouge). Victoria herself never wore make-up at all – except, as is shown in the series, when she experimented during her state visit to the French court in 1843.

The make-up truck for series two of *Victoria* is peppered with historic pictures of Victoria and Albert, their family and associates – drawings, paintings and even some very early photographs. The fact that make-up was looked down upon by aristocrats of the era means that, for the most part, it is kept to a minimum in the series, though the Duke of Cumberland's scar is of course fitted whenever he appears – even though in real life he refused to allow it to be painted and recorded for posterity.

When it came to Victoria's visit to France, however, the team realised that this was a golden opportunity to showcase period make-up, which was accepted more readily at the French court. Nic Collins, the make-up designer, researched products from the period and decided to make powder and rouge from the original recipes, including a beetroot-

stained balm for use on the cheeks. There is a downside to this historical experimentation, however. 'These make-up products don't last,' Nic confides. 'The beetroot balm can only be kept for a few days – women freshly made their make-up for each special occasion.'

Make-up in the early nineteenth century was not a subtle affair, with products like tapioca 'pearl' powder easily noticeable on the skin. It certainly doesn't go down well in the series, with Albert commenting disapprovingly when Victoria experiments with make-up for the first time. To get the look just right, make-up is touched up on set to achieve the best effect for the light, and it can also be adjusted in post-production to increase the red and purple tones.

The team also created all the hair looks for the series, so the trailer is home to a treasure trove of wigs made of human hair. Many of the styles are 'baked' in an oven so they will last for the twelve-hour filming day – a trick that is particularly effective for ringlets. Hairstyles of the period were very complex – Baroness Lehzen's signature nine-stem basket-weave plait, for example, was copied exactly from pictures of the day. When the team discovered that Albert's uncle, Leopold, wore a toupee, they made one for the actor even though he wasn't balding – along

with a fine pair of sideburns. 'Victorian men grew as much hair as they could and then combed it forward to cover bald patches,' Nic explains. 'Wigs were looked on as frivolous. At one stage they were actually taxed.'

Prosthetics are also a team speciality, with the leeches used to bleed Lord Melbourne made on set, including a 'puppet' leech, which was able to 'pulse' to replicate the action of real-life leeches sucking blood. A gruesome gallery of injuries caused by the explosion at the armoury that occurs in the series is also posted on the wall at one side of the truck. One thing's for sure: make-up certainly isn't all about making the actors look pretty.

ORE INTERNATIONAL TRIPS followed in time, with a visit to Germany, Britain's great ally, as well as Belgium and France again in 1845. Victoria and Albert also welcomed distinguished international visitors at Windsor Castle and Buckingham Palace. When the Tsar of Russia visited in June 1844, the young Queen was keen to give a good impression and toured the Tsar's rooms daily in the run-up to his arrival, ensuring that the paintings she'd chosen to entertain him were hung as she'd instructed and the soft furnishings were draped correctly.

Victoria, a proud imperialist, was unashamedly ambitious for her country. As the British Empire expanded, she welcomed its gains and her subsequent sprawl of international dominions, upon which it is famously said 'the sun never set'. British manufacturing was getting ready to take over the world and the British Army and Navy were spearheading the way in what has been described as the biggest land grab in history. The British Raj would shortly take its place in India, with Victoria very firmly at its head, while British gains worldwide would include lands all over Africa and the Middle East.

ALBERT:
That is just the beginning. Uncle Leopold would have a Coburg on every throne in Europe if he could.

HOW ENGLISH IS VICTORIA?

One of the most enduring myths about Victoria, a so-called fact that I encountered many times during the broadcast of the first series for *Victoria*, was that the queen spoke with a German accent. This is emphatically not the case. In fact, at the age of four Princess Victoria told her mother that she wanted to speak English at home, not German. Like the children of immigrants everywhere, she spoke with the accent of her native country, not that of her mother's. Of course she did speak German fluently and she and Albert definitely spoke German together privately, but there is no doubt that Victoria thought in English. Her diary – her most personal document – was always written in English, even though it was larded with German phrases. The notion that Victoria spoke English with a German accent seems to have come from a Monty Python sketch where one of the Pythons played her as a German hausfrau. If nothing else, I can lay that one to rest. It's important because, in England, the charge of being a bunch of Germans is still hurled at the royal family. Indeed, during the First World War, Victoria's grandson George V changed the family name from Saxe-Coburg and Gotha to Windsor, as anti-German feeling was so intense. But in many ways there could be no more English a queen than Victoria. Although her mother and her governess were German, she herself always thought of herself as English and adored stories of her ancestors. She was particularly fond of the Stuarts and used to call herself a Jacobite, which was ironic given that it was her Hanoverian ancestors who had deposed the glamorous Stuarts.

But Victoria did not share the widespread xenophobia of her subjects. She had no qualms about taking a foreign husband, even though the Germans were widely regarded as slow-on-the-uptake sausage-eaters by the British and their press. There would have been a real outcry if Victoria had chosen a French husband as large swathes of the population still remembered the long and bloody Napoleonic wars. (I have tried to show that resentment in the attitude of the Duchess of Buccleuch to France, her brother having been killed at Trafalgar.) The Germans may have been bad but the French were seen as very much worse. So it was a very significant step when Victoria decided to visit France in 1843. She was the first monarch to have left England for nearly a century, and the first to set foot on French soil since Henry VIII. Personally it must have been a revelation; this was the first time she had entered a country of which she was not the monarch, so it must have seemed very strange to her. There is a wonderful story about how she went out incognito one day during her French visit, and was rather put out when nobody recognised her.

One thing I feel quite sure of is that Victoria would have been appalled by Brexit. Victoria and Albert tried to create their own informal European union through strategic marriages of their children. Victoria may have been English to her fingertips, but she understood the value of a family of nations.

HMS TRAFALGAR

BUILT AT THE Royal Dockyard at Woolwich in London and launched in 1841, HMS *Trafalgar* was an enormous 120-gun sailing ship that weighed over 2,500 tons. At Victoria's request the ship was named by Lady Bridport, niece of Lord Nelson, the famed naval commander of the Battle of Trafalgar in 1805. The wine used to launch the *Trafalgar* had come from Nelson's ship, HMS *Victory*, when it returned from battle.

The launch, in June 1841, was a huge event. Five hundred people were aboard the ship when it hit the water – a hundred of them veterans of the battle. In addition, it is estimated that over half a million people turned up to watch from the crowded riverbank or the small boats that peppered the water. Victoria and Albert attended together, and the event was seen at court as a way to restore British public pride despite the ongoing military situation in Afghanistan, where British interests were faring poorly. The painter William Ranwell produced a commemorative painting, and several woodcuts and prints depicting the launch were hastily turned out and sold well. The HMS *Trafalgar* went on to serve at Sebastapol in the Crimean War.

Below: Launch of HMS *Trafalgar* at Woolwich, London, 21 June 1841.

THE HISTORIAN JOHN SEELEY, who was born and died within Victoria's reign, said that the British Empire was 'acquired in a fit of absent-mindedness' and, indeed, there was no over-arching plan. This meant that sometimes disastrous actions were undertaken, like the British intervention in a succession dispute in Afghanistan in 1839, which eventually led to their defeat in 1842 and slashed national pride to pieces. Victoria's salve to the nation was to launch HMS *Trafalgar*, as the Navy was key to Britain's sense of itself as a country and contributed hugely to the empire in an opportunistic fashion. British ships simply proved adept at capturing strategic toeholds that provided jumping-off points for the expansion of British territories. These were captured in different ways and for different reasons, and came under different forms of rule, but what united them was that colonists in all of them sang 'God Save the Queen' in English, in honour of the same woman. Thus Victoria herself became the uniting force of the empire, and British industry was free to make the most of these new markets. Even when some of these countries chose to divest themselves of British rule later in the Victorian era, the changes were largely made by civilised agreement. Australia and Canada both left Victoria on the throne when they gained their independence – indeed, many citizens of those countries are staunch royalists to this day.

Victoria was a contradictory kind of queen. She loved jewels, for example, but was the original aristocrat who was 'too posh to wash'. She enjoyed the company of men, but flew into a rage if her husband so much as chatted to another woman. She loved sex, but was unforgiving in her views on love outside marriage. When Sir Samuel Baker, the great British explorer, naturalist and engineer, returned to London with his Hungarian wife, Florence, Victoria refused to accept Lady Baker at court because she was rumoured to have had sex with her husband before they were married. Given that Sir Samuel had rescued his wife from a slave market, this seems a particularly harsh stance. On the other hand, Victoria's kindness and generosity towards the rescued African slave Sarah Forbes Bonetta (see also pages 252–54) stands in sharp contrast.

LOUIS PHILIPPE:
These handsome Coburg Princes cannot be allowed to found an empire by snapping up all the Queens of Europe.

SARAH FORBES BONETTA

'A gift from the King of the Blacks to the Queen of the Whites.'

KING GEZO OF DAHOMEY

WHEN 30-YEAR-OLD English naval commander Frederick Forbes dropped anchor on the coast of Africa in October 1849, he was on a mission to rid the region of slavery. Slavery had been illegal in British dominions since 1833, but the practice continued in many African states and the British Navy worked against it, 'policing' the seas to stop trafficking wherever possible. Forbes was welcomed at the court of King Gezo, where he witnessed a ritual sacrifice ceremony. One of the slaves to be slaughtered was a small girl of about six years of age. The ritual markings on the child's face signified that she was from a royal line.

Horrified that the child was to be killed, Forbes challenged King Gezo. It is unclear whether he asked for Aina as a gift for his Queen or if Gezo offered her, but the girl left on Forbes's ship, bound for England. In Nigeria she was baptised as 'Sarah Forbes Bonetta'. When Forbes returned to Gravesend, Sarah went to live with his family and the Captain wrote to Queen Victoria, who later met with the little girl at Windsor Castle, where Sarah herself told the Queen about her capture and ordeal.

'I feel myself in duty bound to request their Lordships to lay the offer before Her Majesty, if they should approve thereof. She now passes by the name of "Sarah Bonetta" and is an intelligent, good tempered (I need hardly add Black) girl, about six or seven years of age.'

LETTER FROM CAPTAIN FORBES TO
QUEEN VICTORIA, 3 AUGUST 1850

Sarah continued to live with Forbes's family, though Victoria paid for her education and the little girl came to play at the palace with the royal children. By eight years of age she could speak English well and was learning music. Sarah made friends with Victoria's daughter, Princess Alice, with whom she was particularly close.

'Since her arrival in the country, she has made considerable progress in the study of the English language and manifests great musical talent and intelligence of no common order. Her hair is short, black and curling, strongly indicative of her African birth; while her features are pleasing and handsome, and her manners and conduct most mild and affectionate to all about her.'

LONDON STANDARD OF FREEDOM,
23 NOVEMBER 1850

In 1851, Sarah's health began to suffer and Victoria decided to send her back to Africa, where it was hoped the warm weather would improve her condition. When she left, the Queen ensured that she travelled with adequate and proper clothing and also donated a large cheque to the missionary into whose care Sarah was entrusted. Victoria sent presents regularly to the little girl in her new home and Sarah wrote letters to Victoria and to Alice. In 1855 Sarah returned to England. Later, Victoria would become godmother to Sarah's daughter, though sadly, Sarah died in August 1880 at the age of thirty-seven from tuberculosis.

....

Opposite top: Sarah Forbes Bonetta in 1862. Opposite bottom: Sarah, god-daughter of Queen Victoria, with her husband, James Davies.

ALBERT, FOR HIS part, craved both his wife's attention and her trust, and desperately wanted to be the most important influence in her life to prove himself worthy of sharing her power. Both he and Victoria were diligent in their duties, taking an active part in advising and influencing British politics both at home and abroad, and slowly, Victoria – who had always been quite selfish in getting what she wanted – came to realise how difficult their marriage sometimes was for Albert. After he died she said sadly, 'Will they accept him now?' It is unclear if she meant her aristocratic friends, her subjects or simply the British press, who had vilified the Prince no matter what he undertook. She saw him as a massively talented man who was never really accepted and, loving him as she did, she became his unrelenting champion.

'Never permit people to speak on subjects concerning yourself or your affairs, without your having yourself desired them to do so. The moment a person behaves improperly on this subject, change the conversation.'

~LETTER FROM LEOPOLD, KING OF THE BELGIANS,
TO VICTORIA, 12 JULY 1837

The face that Victoria and Albert presented to the world together, however, was pristine. With their close family life, their dedication to each other and their unprecedented commitment to high culture, technological advancements, philanthropic causes and national life, they projected a powerful image not just as a couple, but as an emblem of Britain. Their subjects knew what they represented both at home and abroad, and Victoria's image (and Albert's too to a lesser extent) became the face of the burgeoning British Empire. When the soon-to-be novelist Charlotte Brontë was in Brussels during the early and mid 1840s, she spotted the Queen, who was also visiting, 'for an instant flashing through the Rue Royale in a carriage and six, surrounded by soldiers. She was laughing and talking very gaily. She looked a little stout, vivacious lady, very plainly dressed, not much dignity or pretension about her.'

ALBERT:
Can you be so naïve that you don't realise that everything you do is political?

BRITAIN'S MILITARY

THE DUKE OF WELLINGTON, military hero of the Battle of Waterloo in 1815, remained the British Army's Commander-in-Chief until 1852 – right through the first decade and a half of Victoria's rule. During his time in office, conditions for ordinary soldiers were greatly improved. The Army had historically been a brutal occupation: it would often mete out harsh penalties for minor infractions, and soldiers received just a shilling a day in pay, but might be charged 'stoppages' for food and clothing. In 1847 a new rule meant that a soldier had to receive at least a penny a day for his service regardless of these 'stoppages'. And a maximum of fifty lashes as punishment for any one soldier was set in 1846 (in 1829 the maximum had been 500 lashes – an astonishing number to endure).

When Lord Howick became Secretary of War in 1835 a new regime also introduced new incentives – good conduct badges and good conduct pay. Howick encouraged investment in rank-and-file soldiers, so, for example, military libraries were set up in many barracks, and for soldiers drawn from the working classes this was a huge incentive – many learned to read during their army service as a result. However, Howick's reforms were not universally popular – he banned free rations of spirits and in place of the daily shot of grog he instituted more hot meals. This improved the well-being of serving soldiers tremendously, even though there was an outcry at being deprived of their drink.

The design and appearence of uniforms changed over Victoria's reign, too. The commonly used 'redcoat' was swapped for a darker uniform, which – like Prince Albert's newly designed helmet (see page 208) – would be less of a target on the battlefield. Changes were also afoot to the kind of weaponry available. The expertise of the Industrial Revolution was not only directed towards factory equipment – new and more efficient guns were important innovations, too.

Despite these developments, Britain in the early Victorian era was less militarised than other powers, including Prussia, Austria and Russia. That said, when combined with the private army of the East India Company, which represented the Crown in India and Southeast Asia, British military might was impressively large. It had little function at home in Britain, though, and as a result did not have as much influence as the armies of other powers.

The British Royal Navy (or 'Senior Service') was larger and more influential than the Army. It was based in Portsmouth and Chatham dockyards and had significant holdings overseas, including Gibraltar, Malta and Bombay. The Navy was key in combating the slave trade and 'policed' seas worldwide, safeguarding Britain's trade routes. The British Empire could not have grown, or indeed functioned, without it. The 'Bombay Marine' was the East India Company's equivalent service and the two forces worked together in the interests of the British Crown.

Internationally, France was viewed as Britain's main enemy and the grudges that had been formed during and after the Napoleonic Wars still lingered. Given the close ties between the British and German royals, Germany was considered an ally (an assumption that would prove disastrous in the early twentieth century after Victoria's death). Still, Britain was not involved in any European wars during the early part of Victoria's reign. Military activity was restricted mainly to keeping the peace and to disastrous interventions in Afghanistan and the successful war against China, which was waged solely to promote Britain's interests in the opium trade.

....

Opposite: Prince Albert in the uniform of his own regiment, 11th Hussars.

H. R. H. Prince Albert.
Prince of Saxe-Coburg and Gotha, etc.

CHAPTER 9
A VERY PUBLIC LIFE

'The wretched creature, not out of his mind, but a thorough scamp ... I hope his trial will be conducted with the greatest strictness.'

···· **LETTER FROM ALBERT TO HIS FATHER, THE DUKE OF SAXE-COBURG AND GOTHA, ON JOHN FRANCIS, 31 MAY 1842** ····

THEN, AS NOW, there were downsides to becoming an icon. As Victoria became more of a national and international figurehead, she also became more of a target. During the Queen's reign there were no less than seven attempts made on her life by thought-to-be assassins. She became the subject of obsessional behaviour, particularly of men – Captain Childers's repeated offers to 'save' Victoria from the 'German' tyranny of Albert was shown in the first series of *Victoria* and is an early example of such behaviour, but there were others, and some of them were even more determined. It was also not unheard of for prostitutes to be asked to 'dress like Her Majesty' and engage in 'right royal role-play' with their clients. Albert attracted his fair share of negative attention, too, including abusive letters, but nobody was to make an attempt on his life.

The Queen's most persistent stalker was known as the Boy Jones (see also pages 262–63), who from the age of fourteen brazenly broke into Buckingham Palace on several occasions between 1838 and 1841. There is no question that security at the palace was initially lax and Jones's incursions meant that this issue was promptly addressed by Prince Albert, who took on extra guards and instigated strict routines for the locking of doors and windows. Jones's interest in the Queen, however, was less threatening and rather more of a nuisance compared to those who fired guns at her, which, in 1842, happened twice within a matter of weeks. When the first assassination attempt was made on Victoria's life in 1840 the man in question, Edward Oxford, was found insane by the court.

THE BOY JONES

EDWARD JONES WAS obsessed with Victoria and how she and the royal family lived. The son of a Westminster tailor, 'the Boy Jones', as he was dubbed, was first arrested aged fourteen in 1838 when he managed to get into the palace disguised as a chimney sweep. A porter caught him in the Marble Hall and gave chase. Jones was captured in St James's Street and was found to have Victoria's underwear stuffed down his trousers. He had also stolen a regimental sword. When asked why he had broken in, he said he'd always wanted to see inside Buckingham Palace and was thinking of writing a book about it.

Then, shortly after Princess Victoria's birth in 1840, Jones once more climbed over the palace wall and got in through an unlocked, unshuttered window. On this occasion, he left without being caught, which suggests there may well have been other occasions when he visited the palace and nobody detected him. A few days after this break-in he came back again and was caught under a sofa in Victoria's dressing room by Baroness Lehzen.

It was, of course, alarming to Prince Albert that Jones had gained access to the palace with such ease when there was a new baby in the nursery and the Queen was particularly vulnerable. To limit the publicity surrounding this lack of security at the palace, Jones was tried in secret and sentenced to three months in a house of correction. But he didn't give up! Almost as soon as he was released in March 1841, he broke back into Buckingham Palace and was caught eating stolen food from a table in the royal apartments. He was also caught on two further occasions, sitting on the throne. This time he was sentenced to hard labour. When he was released he was offered a large sum of money (four pounds a week) to appear on stage in a music hall production, but he refused. Instead, he was caught loitering near the palace.

The Establishment (Albert included) decided to turn to the Navy for help. Jones was kidnapped (or, as it was called, 'pressed into service') and sent overseas. Despite a tour to Brazil, he turned up in London again and the Navy incarcerated him in a prison ship for six years, eventually deporting him to Australia.

It was because of Jones that new security measures were adopted within the palace and extra guards put in place. Prince Albert oversaw these arrangements himself. The Boy Jones, in time, became a running joke in newspapers and magazines, and the story of his obsession with Victoria followed him all his life. Later, Jones became an alcoholic and a burglar, and, despite returning to the UK after his deportation, he eventually settled in Perth, Australia, where he became the town crier. Even there, he was persecuted by jokes about his younger days, and his brother reported that these jokes annoyed him tremendously.

....

Opposite right: Boy Jones. Opposite left: One of many assassination attempts on the Queen.

THE ILLUSTRATED LONDON NEWS

REGISTERED AT THE GENERAL POST-OFFICE FOR TRANSMISSION

No. 2236.—VOL. LXXX.

SATURDAY, MARCH 11, 1882.

THE PRISONER

THE PISTOL

THE BULLET ON LARGER SCALE

ATTEMPT TO SHOOT THE QUEEN AT THE WINDSOR RAILWAY STATION.—SEE PAGE 224.

FROM A SKETCH SUPPLIED BY MR. BURNSIDE, PHOTOGRAPHER.

RETURN OF THE BOY JONE
OR, THE WHIG JONESES AND THEIR LEADER.

SIR ROBERT PEEL: I wonder, Ma'am, given the considerable discontent among the lower orders at the moment, if a ball might be misconstrued.

ON 29 MAY 1842, Albert spotted a man pulling a gun and levelling it at the Queen while the royal couple were on a short carriage ride from Buckingham Palace to the Chapel Royal at St James's Palace. He didn't fire, but Albert was adamant that the threat was real and he was alarmed enough to make a plan. Victoria and Albert decided jointly not to change their routine and to try to 'draw out' this potential assassin the next day, with two equerries riding close to the carriage as an extra security measure. And sure enough, on 30 May, at around six in the evening, 20-year-old John Francis, the son of a machine maker, stood on Constitution Hill waiting for the royal couple to return to the palace in their barouche from a drive on Hampstead Heath. Francis drew his flintlock and a police constable named Tanner, who was on duty (and had been alerted to be vigilant), bravely rushed towards the would-be assassin and knocked the gun from his hand. The shot fired but did not hurt anyone – neither the Queen or the Prince, nor the policeman or any of the public nearby.

Francis was unrepentant. When he was taken into custody he said, 'Damn the Queen! Why should she be such an expense to the nation?' And despite the public outrage at his actions, there was some sympathy towards Francis's statement – the country's finances were, after all, in a parlous state. Sir Robert Peel had just imposed the first income tax ever to be levied in peacetime on incomes exceeding £150 a year and the Corn Laws were driving up food prices and causing political unrest across the country. And at the same time Victoria had announced her intention to throw the lavish masked Plantagenet Ball 'to stimulate trade' (see pages 224–5), a move that looked dangerously like profligacy.

NIGEL LINDSAY

PLAYS

SIR ROBERT PEEL

'Peel was quite a fusty, prosaic man, used to dealing with people older than Victoria. In the second series Peel is at the height of his powers at a very exciting time in English history and that's very interesting to play. I think Peel realised Victoria was so much more than her stature and her age. I think he saw that, whereas politicians come and go, the monarch was the one stable force.'

SIR ROBERT PEEL

'A cold, odd man.'

···· VICTORIA'S JOURNAL, ON SIR ROBERT PEEL, 8 MAY 1839 ····

INITIALLY, VICTORIA DIDN'T like Sir Robert Peel, the Tory prime minister who took over from Lord Melbourne in 1841. Lord Melbourne had been her favourite and she saw Peel as a usurper. However, Albert supported Sir Robert and gradually Victoria changed her mind about him. This may be, in part, because Lord Melbourne passed on tips to Peel on how to approach the Queen, advising him to explain clearly the reasons for anything he had to propose: 'She likes having things explained … in detail … shortly and clearly,' he said. Melbourne also advised Peel not to irritate Victoria by talking about religion.

At first Peel was shy with the Queen. He had a habit of fidgeting, which Victoria said reminded her of a dancing master. However, by the end of Peel's term as prime minister, he had gained her affection and a bond had formed between them. Stepping down and leaving the Queen was, he said, 'one of the most painful moments' of his life.

Peel's time in office had a huge effect in many spheres. He set up the Metropolitan Police Force at Scotland Yard in 1829 – the constables were known as 'bobbies', named after him – essentially making him the father of the modern police force. As prime minister, he oversaw several reforms to employment in factories, limiting working hours for women and children. And as a committed Anglican, he was also moved by the Irish Potato Famine (see pages 284–5) and set himself to repealing the Corn Laws (see pages 268–9) so that food aid could be delivered to Ireland, splitting his own party in the process. And in a dramatic turn of events, Peel was also the target of an assassination attempt that resulted in the accidental killing of Edward Drummond, his personal secretary, in 1843. London was shocked by this attempt and huge crowds turned out to mourn Drummond.

Peel was only prime minister for six years in total – over two terms – but his influence was huge and his political career overall spanned two decades. He is credited with creating the modern Conservative Party and is one of the nineteenth century's most influential politicians. After his death in 1850, a statue was erected to his memory in Parliament Square in London. He had five children with his wife, Julia, and their four sons all went on to have distinguished political or military careers.

THE CORN LAWS

'I maintain that the existing corn laws are bad, because they have given a monopoly of food to the landed interest over every other class and over every other interest in the kingdom.'

DOCTOR AND RADICAL MP JOSEPH HUME

THE CORN LAWS ran from 1815 to 1846 and imposed restrictions and tariffs on imported grain to keep prices high for domestic producers. This meant the price of food was higher than it needed to be in early Victorian Britain. Many ordinary people opposed the Corn Laws and when the Anti-Corn Law League was set up in 1839, sponsored by rich Whig supporters, it focused on opposition to the Corn Laws, calling meetings and lobbying politicians, voters and press interest.

Sir Robert Peel tackled the Corn Laws in 1842, modifying the sliding scale of charges on imports of grain. Later, as the Irish Potato Famine became increasingly acute in 1845 (see also pages 284–5), he decided to go further. Peel was not popular among his own back-bench MPs at Westminster and his Conservative Party was made up of many supporters with farming interests, but so dire was the situation in Ireland, the Irish Famine meant that he was prepared to risk splitting his own party and endangering his own position as prime minister.

This, in fact, is exactly what happened – while some Conservatives backed Peel's moral stand on the Corn Laws and the vote he forced through to repeal them, almost half his party voted against him and the bill was only passed thanks to a minority of his own Conservatives and a majority of the Whig (Liberal) opposition and some independent free traders. In June 1846, the bill was then pushed through the House of Lords by the Duke of Wellington. Soon after this break with his own party, Peel's Irish Coercion Bill – intended to suppress the agitation that was brewing in Ireland – was defeated in the Commons, and Peel felt forced to resign immediately.

....

Opposite: A caricature lambasting British Prime Minister Robert Peel for his stance on the Corn Laws which placed duties on imported and exported grain.

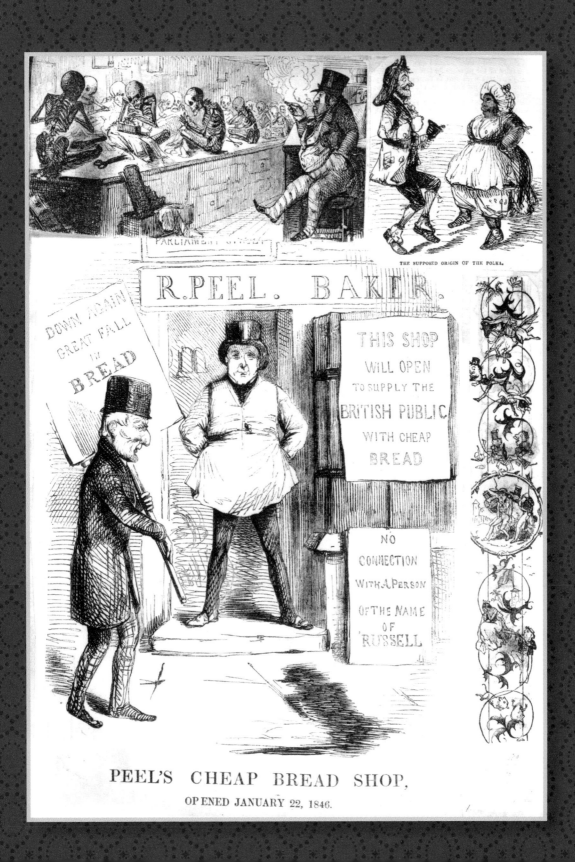

PARLIAMENT STREET

THE SUPPOSED ORIGIN OF THE POLKA.

R. PEEL. BAKER.

DOWN AGAIN GREAT FALL IN BREAD

THIS SHOP WILL OPEN TO SUPPLY THE BRITISH PUBLIC WITH CHEAP BREAD

NO CONNECTION WITH A PERSON OF THE NAME OF RUSSELL

PEEL'S CHEAP BREAD SHOP,
OPENED JANUARY 22, 1846.

WHEN VICTORIA GOT back to the palace after the gun incident she first ran to tell Baroness Lehzen what had happened, then she informed the rest of her family. Her uncles rallied round in support, but perhaps the young Queen didn't need it. In her diary entry that night she sounds almost breathless with excitement. 'They all said it was very brave of me to have gone out, knowing, as we did, for certain, since the morning that this man was about. I felt quite agitated & excited.' She declared, 'When I think of what might have happened, I shudder!'

Victoria's uncles were not the only ones who were impressed by her nerve; the day after Francis's assassination attempt, Londoners turned out to cheer her bravery when she took her usual carriage ride in the afternoon. Victoria refused to be cowed by any assassination attempts made on her life and the public loved her for it. Her uncle, Count Emmanuel Mensdorff-Pouilly, insisted on riding with her when she went out the following day, and from then on a detail of Metropolitan Police followed the Queen wherever she went. The decision on how and where she would travel always rested with Victoria, though, and she took the attitude that she would not be kept a prisoner in the palace. That evening when she attended the opera she recorded that 'the whole House rose, cheered, & waved their hats & handkerchiefs. "God save the Queen" was sung & there was immense applause at the end of each verse.' The public certainly appreciated Victoria's pluck.

'It now only remains for me to pass upon you the sentence of the law, which is that you, John Francis . . . be hanged by the neck until you be dead . . .'

JUDGE'S REMARKS AT THE TRIAL OF JOHN FRANCIS, AS REPORTED IN THE *SHEFFIELD INDEPENDENT*, 25 JUNE 1842

DUCHESS OF KENT:
But Victoria is
a tempest.

JUST OVER A fortnight later, Francis appeared in court, charged on four counts, including high treason, and was found guilty. He was sentenced to death by being hanged and quartered – the traditional (medieval) sentence for regicide being to be hanged, drawn (tortured) and quartered (cut into pieces). On hearing what was to happen to Francis, Edward Oxford, who had shot at the Queen two years before, remarked that had he been hanged, this second attempt would never have been made. However, it was generally felt that the death sentence was too harsh a penalty even for an attempt on the Queen's life, given that Francis had nowhere near succeeded. There were also reservations among the Establishment that if a man was hanged for a failed attempt, future juries might be unwilling to convict for the same offence because the death penalty seemed too great a price. In the end, Victoria commuted Francis's sentence to transportation to Australia for life and he was sent across the world to face a long term of hard labour in a penal colony. Quickly, Sir Robert Peel brought forward an Act of Parliament that changed the legal view of an attempt on the life of the reigning monarch from high treason to 'high misdemeanour'. This meant that in future the penalty was reduced to a term of imprisonment and a sentence of whipping.

That summer, the gossiping classes talked of little else but Francis's attempt on the Queen's life and how it had been averted, and despite his comments on his arrest, the newspapers pronounced that the Queen's assassin was not driven by revolutionary desire but by a 'diseased craving for notoriety' instead. In an elegant new security measure, Albert designed Victoria a parasol armed with chainmail, though it is unknown whether she carried this with her when she ventured out in her carriage.

'Lord Abinger said, he should be doing a violence to his own feelings, and to the feelings of all who heard him, if he did not pass upon him the heaviest sentence the common law of the land allows …'

~JUDGE'S REMARKS AT THE TRIAL OF JOHN WILLIAM BEAN,
AS REPORTED IN *THE SUFFOLK CHRONICLE*; OR *WEEKLY GENERAL
ADVERTISER & COUNTY EXPRESS*, SATURDAY,
27 AUGUST 1842

THE SECOND ATTEMPT made on the Queen's life that summer took place on 3 July, when Victoria and Albert were driving in a carriage along the Mall. John William Bean, who was described as a 'humpback' wearing a long, brown coat, pushed his way to the front of the crowd that had assembled to wave at the royal couple, and pulled out a pistol. A sixteen-year-old boy standing near him, Charles Edward Dassett, grabbed hold of Bean's wrist and dragged the assailant across the road, where he told two policemen what had happened. For whatever reason, the officers, Hearn and Claxton, did not take the incident seriously and dismissed the valiant young vigilante, letting Bean go.

A few hours later, Dassett was apprehended in Green Park for having a pistol in his hand – the one he had taken from Bean. He again told the story of what had happened and this time the police went on the hunt for other witnesses. Hearn and Claxton were suspended from duty for not taking action, and when other witnesses came forward Dassett was released. That evening, police arrested Bean at his father's house in Clerkenwell. Several newspapers reported that he had written a letter, which declared that he might not 'see his father again; that he would not do anything dishonest, but he might because desperate, & signing himself "Your unhappy & disobedient son"'.

When arrested, Bean was contrite, saying he had waited for three days to take his shot, but had not intended to hurt the Queen, as he had only loaded the gun with paper and gunpowder and had pointed it at the ground. He was presumably hoping to be transported, just like Francis.

CROWD SCENES/EXTRAS

'There were a huge amount of actors and big scenes, which everyone would be in, and they each had to look right.'

ROSALIND EBBUTT, COSTUME DESIGNER

Many of the supporting artists on the set of season two of *Victoria* are regulars hired from local agencies. They need to arrive on set ready to be made up as real Victorians – and occasionally there have been problems when an extra arrives and looks nothing like their photograph. On one occasion, someone turned up with their hair dyed blue, so they had to come back once the dye had been washed out. In general, it's best if extras don't have tattoos, a tan or highlighted, coloured or close-cut hair – and anyone with a shaved head is out!

Lots of extras have other, regular part-time jobs or are retired. Shooting days are long and there is a lot of sitting around, waiting until you're needed, so patience is also a requirement. Everyone has to turn up in the morning, even if they aren't needed till later, so it's not unusual to see footmen or housemaids on their laptops, knitting, reading or talking on their mobile phones. Luckily there is always tea and coffee available on set for those who are waiting around, and a catering truck provides breakfasts and lunches over the course of the day. If a background character becomes established even in a non-speaking part, they cannot take part in other crowd scenes – so for some extras it's once a kitchen maid, always a kitchen maid.

When it's time to go on set, the costumes, hair and make-up must be exactly right. Shooting a historical drama makes filming a longer process while all of this important detail is meticulously checked. Every extra is photographed from different angles so that the look can be exactly reproduced if part of a scene has to be reshot.

It's common for up to eighty supporting artists to be required either on set or on location for big crowd scenes. Anything larger and the CGI team are brought in to create the illusion of more people. Individual extras are shot from different angles against a green screen and then 'dropped' into the background, their image altered slightly in each incarnation.

Special effects in historical drama are about recreating history. As visual effects producer Louise Hastings explains, 'The effects need to be invisible to transport the audience back to the Victorian era.' It all has to look absolutely authentic and real. For sweeping scenes of old London, for example, the CGI team used maps and old paintings for reference, then added in horses, carriages and chimney smoke, as well as crowds on the streets, to recreate the capital city as it was 170 years ago.

Right: Sir Robert Peel.

VICTORIA ONLY HEARD of Bean's thwarted attempt afterwards. She was told by the MP Sir James Graham, who visited the Queen after she had returned to Buckingham Palace and had eaten her lunch. 'How mad and strange all this is!' she declared. 'But how providence watches over us.' She claimed to have had a premonition of the attack and had remarked to Albert as they walked in Buckingham Palace Gardens only two days before that she felt another attempt on her life was imminent. The next day, when Sir Robert Peel visited the Queen, he reputedly wept, thinking of what might have happened. Victoria herself was more pragmatic, dismissing Bean's attempt and saying the gun would never have caused much damage, not being properly loaded. She also seems to have taken a certain glee in the fact that Bean was considered very ugly by all those who wrote reports of him. His trial lasted just six hours. He was found guilty and sentenced to eighteen months in Newgate prison.

THE CHARTISTS

'*Every noble work is at first impossible.*'

PHILOSOPHER, HISTORIAN AND CHARTIST THOMAS CARLYLE

THE CHARTIST MOVEMENT was a working-class movement for democratic political reform that ran from 1838 to 1848. It was named after the People's Charter, which called for wider voting rights, secret ballots in elections, payment of MPs, constituency reform and abolition of the requirement for MPs to be men of property. Millions of people signed their names in support of the Charter and huge mass meetings were held across the country. Some newspapers supported the movement and articles were read out in workplaces, public houses and at meetings for the benefit of the illiterate.

The House of Commons' repeated refusal to hear the petitioners resulted in a furious backlash, leading to strikes, riots and insurrection. In 1842 hundreds of arrests were made as the uprisings broke out. Though the national executive of the Chartist movement was found not guilty, many supporters were imprisoned or transported. In fact, many Chartists who were transported in this period continued to militate in British colonies and achieved reform there.

The Chartists also agitated against the Church of England and campaigned for a separation of Church and State and an end to huge wages for senior bishops and dignitaries. Even a Chartist hymnbook was commissioned, containing hymns about social injustice.

In 1847 a Chartist MP was finally elected and in 1848 a mass meeting was organised at Kennington Common. The Chartists claimed at this point that they had a total of 6 million signatures for the Charter, though government officials put the figure at 1.9 million. Either way, given that 1848 was a year of huge political instability all across Europe and there were revolts against the monarchies of Germany, France, Italy, Sicily, Switzerland, Hungary, Poland, Ukraine, Romania and the Austrian Empire, the Chartist movement was particularly alarming for Victoria.

Ultimately, though, the movement was unsuccessful and it disbanded. By the end of Victoria's reign, however, many of the reforms the Chartists had pushed for had come about in political life and Britain had achieved change – without a revolution.

....

Left: Mass meeting of Chartists on Kennington Common, 1 January 1848.
Below: Cartoon of Chartists' attempt to force a giant charter through Parliament.

IN THESE EARLY years of the couple's reign, all was not well beyond the palace walls – Chartism was on the rise, social conditions were poor, the Potato Famine was decimating the Irish population and across Europe revolutions were brewing. Victoria's strength in the face of these attempts was an important factor in bringing the public onside and rallying ordinary citizens to the royal cause. It would be difficult not to admire the young Queen's pluck even if you didn't support Sir Robert Peel's income tax or the expenditure passed by Parliament to keep up the Royal Household. Nonetheless, Albert made sure that staff, police officers and military units were increasingly aware of the risk to the royals as they went about their daily lives and that they were primed to take action. It was almost a decade before another attempt was made on the Queen's life.

DR TRAILL:
I saw a woman
die today, Anne.
Of starvation. She
left five children.

VICTORIAN POLICEMEN
(By courtesy of Mr. A. J. Moore)

Above: A line of 'Peelers'.

THE IRISH POTATO FAMINE

'The Almighty sent the potato blight but the English created the Famine.'

IRISH ACTIVIST, AUTHOR AND JOURNALIST JOHN MITCHEL

THE IRISH POTATO Famine started in 1845 when the first potato crops failed in Ireland. Potato blight was endemic across Europe in this period, but the famine hit hardest in Ireland mainly because the situation was not managed competently, either by the government at Westminster or by the absentee landlords of the Irish estates. About a third of the Irish population relied on potatoes as their main source of food, but most were tenants with little right over the land they farmed, and as a result they had few reserves to help them through the hard times. Grain was also grown in Ireland, but this was reserved for export and the price was protected by the Corn Laws (see pages 268–9). When the Corn Laws were repealed by the Prime Minister, Sir Robert Peel, in 1846, the price of corn plummeted, as did the price of agricultural land and labour.

'In company with Dr Traill, the Rector of Schull, I met Dr McCormick, the dispensary physician of the parish of Kilmoe; he stated that on Tuesday, March 9, he had met a man, a father, tottering along the road – a rope was over his shoulder, and at the other end of the rope, streeling along the ground, were two dead children, whom he was with difficulty dragging to the grave.'

Dr Traill, a protestant rector from Schull in Cork, tried to persuade local landlords to keep their grain in Ireland and save seed potatoes for use. He also wrote to the British government, giving an eye-witness account of what was going on and appealing for help. Traill tried his best to help his congregation and those beyond their number living in the area, but there were simply too many people in need and he had few resources. In real life, he didn't visit Buckingham Palace, as is depicted in the series.

At first the government responded to the famine by setting up soup kitchens, instituting new workhouses and starting a programme of public works, but these had a limited effect and, in fact, slowed public charitable donation as it was felt that the taxpayer was taking care of the situation. As the famine progressed Victoria herself sent a £2,000 donation and wrote a 'queen's letter' to promote the fundraising drive, and suggested instituted 'fast' days to draw attention to the issue, but none of this eased the situation and the message sent by government action continued to be mixed. When America sent a ship of grain to feed the Irish, for example, British customs officers impounded it, claiming it would disturb trade. It has been calculated that there was enough grain available to mitigate the famine's effect in Ireland but these resources were simply not distributed. The prevailing political doctrine of the day was the market should be left to find its own level. This was disastrous for those in Ireland who were now starving to death, and as the crisis grew there was a dogmatic refusal at Westminster to accept that government policy was not working.

IN A STUBBLE FIELD.

> *'I saw the dying, the living and the dead lying indiscriminately on the same floor.'*
>
> ARTIST JAMES MAHONEY, CORK, AN EYE WITNESS TO THE FAMINE

Within a couple of years of the blight hitting Ireland, absentee landlords started to order their agents to evict tenants for non-payment of rent. This made the situation worse and furious Irish activists took violent revenge on landlords and landlords' agents – several were murdered. At home, as the suffering rolled on, the British public had their sympathies dulled by 'famine fatigue', fuelled by the public view that the Irish Catholic population were indolent and had too many children. The press portrayed the Irish as freeloaders who lacked self-reliance, and day after day headlines reported the famine as an act of providence.

Ultimately, a million Irish citizens died from starvation, malnutrition or diseases associated with lack of food. Many more emigrated. The famine has become a folk memory and Queen Victoria is known in Ireland as the 'Famine Queen'. Victoria visited Ireland after the famine in 1849, and though the Viceroy did his best to protect her from the reality of the situation, she noted that 'men are very poorly, often raggedly dressed'. It was quickly recognised that government action could and should have been more effective and that although Peel had done his best he walked an unsteady line between his own conscience and the hard-line political view that the market must be allowed to run its own course, which, sadly, was the attitude that prevailed.

....
Left: Scenes of the Irish Potato Famine.

DR TRAILL

One of the challenges of writing *Victoria* is trying to make the political turmoil of the 1840s relevant to a modern audience. My approach is to try to find the personal story that illustrates the political reality. When it came to the Potato Famine in Ireland, I had a personal interest. My great-great-great-grandfather, Dr Robert Traill, was the rector of Schull, a small town in County Cork, in the 1840s, and had a vital role to play in the Irish Potato Famine.

Dr Traill was an evangelical Protestant who went to the Catholic southwest hoping to convert what he called the 'papist heathen'. He was not successful. The Catholic peasantry revolted against paying tithes to the Protestant Church of Ireland – they burnt an effigy of Traill outside the church and threw burning torches at the rectory. Traill, his wife Anne and their five children lived under virtual house arrest in a fortified rectory, completely estranged from the native population. But when the first signs of the potato blight appeared in 1845, Traill, who had spent the last ten years translating the Hebrew historian Josephus' account of the Jewish revolt against Roman rule, found awful echoes of the biblical famine in the countryside outside his door.

Although he had hardly spoken to a Catholic before this point, Traill was so horrified by the suffering around him that he decided it was his mission to make the government in England realise just how catastrophic the failure of the potato harvest was to the Irish peasantry. His letters to *The Irish Times* are masterpieces of impassioned rhetoric. Traill says that if the government does not send relief, 'then many more will be blotted from the book of being'. Traill's stand was not popular with his superiors in the Church of Ireland, who felt rather as the English government did, that the Catholic peasantry had brought this misfortune upon themselves by relying too heavily upon potatoes. But unlike many of his Protestant colleagues, Traill did not offer food in return for attendance at his church – a practice that came to be known as 'souperism'; instead, he sent his wife and children to Dublin, joined forces with a local Catholic priest and turned his rectory into a soup kitchen that fed everyone in his parish, regardless of their religious denomination. It was a remarkable change of heart.

The failure of the potato crop had a devastating effect on Ireland; its population, which was eight million in 1840, had more than halved by the end of the decade – a drop caused by death and mass emigration to the New World. Traill himself died of famine fever in 1847. After he passed away, the Church of Ireland sued his wife for damage to the rectory.

....

Opposite: Dr Traill with a dying man in Schull, 1847, plus scenes during the Potato Famine.

German —
an English —
Berlin.

VICTORIA
...oes to Berlin.

perhaps puts a hand

VICTORIA 2 - EP 2 LILAC

1   EXT. BUCKINGHAM P...

Palace just begin...
CLOSE on SENTRY - ...

2   EXT. BUCKINGHAM P...

A small hand come...
a boy of about th...
the BOY JONES. Sm... for his age, bright eyes and cheeky,
confident. He isn't in rags, but we know at once that he is
an intruder. It's clear from the ease with which he scales
the wall that he has done this many times before. He jumps to
th... ...und: we see that he knows exactly where he is going.
                                                    CUT TO:

3   I...

So, as I d...
have arranged to ...
Society. Sir Robert say-
meet Charles Babbage, who has
developed a most intriguing...

VICTORIA
(cutting him off)
But why do you have to go out? Why
can't your Mr. Cabbage come here?

ALBERT looks past her into the drawing room.
with MR. BUMPS and WILHELMINA builds a card
ERNEST. The DUCHESS is looking at fashion pl

EPILOGUE:
A ROYAL LEGACY

'It is you who have entirely formed me.'

···· LETTER FROM VICTORIA TO ALBERT, 8 SEPTEMBER 1844 ····

VICTORIA AND ALBERT were as dedicated a royal couple as had ever been seen. Their marriage, like those of their forebears, was originally brokered with dynastic alliances in mind rather than romance, but it grew into something altogether different – a loving and united front, based on the shared principles of family, duty and hard work, the like of which had been rare in royal families.

Despite their differences in personality, despite the arguments and despite the ongoing power struggles, Victoria and Albert had a relationship based on mutual love, passion and a deep-seated desire to take on the business of ruling and to do so well. It was never easy, and it took time, but eventually they found a balance and made it work. Together, they formed a unit, projecting an unassailable image of domestic harmony and playing to each of their strengths to embrace modernity, navigate social and political unrest and expand their influence – and that of Britain – throughout their burgeoning empire.

1854

'They call him slow because he does not gamble, does not use offensive language, and does not keep an opera dancer.'

LETTER TO *THE TIMES* FROM A MEMBER OF THE PUBLIC,
IN ALBERT'S DEFENCE, 1854

THE YEARS FROM 1841 to 1846, which series two of *Victoria* covers, were when the royal marriage established itself – the couple's first five children were born, Albert made his improvements to the royal properties and households and staked out his influence. Even Victoria – a person who always knew what she wanted (one visitor to her schoolroom in Kensington Palace recalled that the Princess would not share her toys) – eventually learned to share with Albert. It took about six years from the day of their marriage to the point in 1846 when the Queen noted in her diary that she had misunderstood how awful it must have been for Albert when he first came to Buckingham Palace, and how guilty she felt for not only allowing herself other influences, but also for not realising how superior Albert's advice was to that of the confidantes she had turned to before. Her early concerns about his sphere of political influence and power eventually dissipated, and the couple began to operate as one.

Right: Portrait of the Prince Consort,
Prince Albert of Saxe-Coburg and Gotha.

VICTORIA:
He thinks he would
do it better.

MELBOURNE:
He would not be
the first man to
underestimate
a woman.

ALBERT HAD INDEED managed to prove himself – not only personally, as a husband who could never quite be master in his own home, but also on the world stage, as the Queen's consort. Ever the outsider as far as the British aristocracy was concerned, he had used sheer determination and intellect to win over many of his critics – including Lord Melbourne, who shook off his initial reservations about Albert's 'indifference to the ladies' (it was thought best that a young prince should sow his wild oats prior to marriage), and quickly became impressed by his work ethic and capacity for reason. However, these were not qualities generally admired by the *beau monde* at court. The upper classes remained watchful of this Prince who was socially awkward, rarely drank alcohol and didn't enjoy hunting, but British politicians quickly realised that going to Albert first before seeking the Queen's opinion was an effective way of smoothing the passage of ideas. Having initially rejected Victoria's request for Albert to be titled Prince Consort and paid a stipend in line with other royal men, Parliament voted in these measures in 1857, once he had proved himself.

'You will find as your children grow up that as a rule your children are a bitter disappointment – their greatest object being to do precisely what their parents do not wish and have anxiously tried to prevent.'

~LETTER FROM VICTORIA TO HER DAUGHTER, VICTORIA,
THE PRINCESS ROYAL, 5 JANUARY 1876

IN THE MID 1840S, with their domestic life established, the nursery flourishing and the building of Osborne House underway, the royal couple began to travel, boosting the image of the British monarchy. They visited Prussia, Belgium, France and several German states, including Albert's home of Coburg, over the next fifteen years or so. From this power base they planned to extend the reach of the House of Saxe-Coburg and Gotha across Europe by marrying their children into other royal houses, thus creating a pan-European royal concord. Beyond Britain, the institution of royalty was in crisis and the continent was fractious, with frequent uprisings and wars breaking out, including revolutions in 1848 in Sicily, Italy, the Austrian Empire, France and Germany. Victoria and Albert had ambitions to heal these wounds.

As the royal nursery grew, the royal couple determined that they would educate their eldest son, Bertie, to be a model British king. As it turned out, Bertie had more in common with his louche Hanoverian forebears than his father, and the concerted efforts of both his parents could not tame his love of pleasure. Victoria wrote to her daughter, Victoria, the Princess Royal, that she couldn't understand what had gone wrong. 'This is inexplicable and very annoying!' she raged, completely unable to accept that she herself had rebelled against her own mother's plans for her. Both Victoria and Albert despaired of their eldest son and never got to see that, in the end, he actually made a surprisingly good king when he eventually came to the throne in 1901.

THEIR PLAN TO create a peaceful, united Europe ruled over by their descendants also failed to materialise. Victoria's uncle, Leopold, King of the Belgians, had backed this idea, seeing the European royal houses as a huge breeding ground for influence and the nursery at Buckingham Palace as full of potential. But history did not fall in with Victoria and Albert's plans, and with two devastating world wars rending Europe apart within forty years of Victoria's death, and the Russian Revolution that saw one of her granddaughters and five of her great-grandchildren murdered in 1918, the British royal family stayed, in the main, resolutely British.

'Everything [is] always made so uncomfortable for Kings and Queens.'
~VICTORIA IN CONVERSATION WITH LORD MELBOURNE
BEFORE SHE MARRIED ALBERT, 10 FEBRUARY 1840

Victoria and Albert's royal legacy does live on, however. Many of the traditions they instituted are still in use, including the way royal births are announced, royal Christmas traditions and the family's love of Scotland. Overall, the monarchy as we know it today, with its emphasis on ordinary family life, philanthropy, duty and stability – with a good dose of pomp and ceremony thrown in – owes a great deal to the model that Victoria and Albert created. Their love affair seems refreshingly modern and glamorous to this day, with its ups and downs, its temper tantrums, its lavish gifts, its struggles for equality and its basis in deep sexual attraction. It was also one of the strongest weapons in the couple's arsenal to engage the British people with the possibilities of a modern monarchy. They were the most privileged couple of their age, the most famous of lovers and the best of friends.

CAST LIST

Jenna Coleman – Queen Victoria

Rufus Sewell – Lord Melbourne

Tom Hughes – Prince Albert

Catherine Flemming – Duchess of Kent

Daniela Holtz – Baroness Louise Lehzen

Adrian Schiller – Penge

Tommy Lawrence Knight – Brodie

Nell Hudson – Miss Skerrett

Margaret Clunie – Harriet, Duchess
of Sutherland

Anna Wilson-Jones – Lady Emma Portman

Peter Firth – Duke of Cumberland

Peter Bowles – Duke of Wellington

Nigel Lindsay – Sir Robert Peel

Pete Ivatts – Archbishop of Canterbury

Tom Price – Duke of Sutherland

Alex Jennings – Leopold

David Oakes – Prince Ernest

Jordan Waller – Lord Alfred Paget

Andrew Bicknell – Duke of Coburg

Ferdinand Kingsley – Charles Francatelli

Jasper Jacob – Lord Chamberlain

Samantha Colley – Eliza Skerrett

Bebe cave – Wilhelmina Coke

Tommy Rodger – Boy Jones

Leo Suter – Albert Drummond

Diana Rigg – Duchess of Buccleuch

Tilly Steele – Cleary

Phil Rowson – John Bright

Emerald Fennell – Ada Lovelace

Peter Forbes – Craddock

Alexander Owen – Dr Brydon

Robin Soans – Sir James Clark

Thomas Padden – William Fothergill Cooke

Henry Faber – Montpensier

Antonia Desplat – Hortense

Dan Fredenburgh – Chadwick

Ashley Zhangazha – Ira Aldridge

Jo Stone-Fewings – Babbage

Hebe Beardsall – Princess Alda

Jacob Krichefski – Nathaniel Bascombe

Gavin Marshall – George Combe

Nick Waring – James Planche

Martha West – Miss Penge

Andrew Neil – Crofter

Martin Compston – Dr Traill

Grainne Keenan – Mrs Traill

PICTURE CREDITS

Main Victoria series photography by Gareth Gatrell © Mammoth Screen Limited 2017. Scotland unit photography by Mark Mainz © Mammoth Screen Limited 2017. All other images © Shutterstock.com, with the exception of the following:

Illustrated London News Ltd/Mary Evans Picture Library p283 middle; © Sam Hew/Mary Evans Picture Library ; p181 top left; 2d Alan King/Alamy Stock Photo p127 top; Andrew Fare/Alamy Stock Photo p236; Antiques & Collectables/Alamy Stock Photo p153 top ; Art Collection 2/Alamy Stock Photo p116 right; Art Collection 3/Alamy Stock Photo p67 bottom; ART Collection/Alamy Stock Photo p115; ART collection/ Alamy Stock Photo p162; Bournemouth News and Picture Service p261 right; British Library, London, UK/© British Library Board. All Rights Reserved/Bridgeman Images p37 top, 64 right; British Museum, London, UK / Bridgeman Images p156; Camille Silvy/Hulton Archive/Getty Images p251 bottom; Château de Versailles, France/Bridgeman Images p292; Chronicle/Alamy Stock Photo p51, 89 bottom, 105 top, 147, 185, 190, 219 bottom, 223 top, 225, 261 left, 281, 283 top; Classic Image/Alamy Stock Photo p119, 276; Contraband Collection/Alamy Stock Photo p92 top; David Pearson Collection/ Mary Evans Picture Library p155; De Luan/Alamy Stock Photo p285 top right; Everett Collection Historical/Alamy Stock Photo p111; GL Archive/Alamy Stock Photo p18, 215 bottom; Granger Historical Picture Archive/Alamy Stock Photo p64 left, 89 top, 142 middle, 153 bottom, 181 bottom left; Granger Historical Picture Archive/ Alamy Stock Photo p285 top left; Heritage Image Partnership Ltd/Alamy Stock Photo p132, 161, 232, 110; Hilary Morgan/Alamy Stock Photo p25, p35; Historical Images Archive/Alamy Stock Photo p153 middle, 181 top right; Hulton Archive/Getty Images p142 top, p267; Hulton Archive/Stringer/Getty Images; p239; iÐÐÐlbusca/istock/Getty Images p92 bottom; IMAGEPAST/Alamy Stock Photo p105 bottom; INTERFOTO/Alamy Stock Photo p94, 131; Jeff Morgan 10/Alamy Stock Photo p201; Lordprice Collection/ Alamy Stock Photo p127 bottom, 255; Mary Evans Picture Library p183, 235 right, 279 bottom, Royal coat of arms of Queen Victoria (on pages 125, 128, 143, 186); Mary Evans/Natural History Museum p76; National Railway Museum, York, North Yorkshire, UK/Bridgeman Images p211; Newberry Library, Chicago, Illinois, USA/Bridgeman Images p37 bottom; Niday Picture Library/Alamy Stock Photo p223 bottom; Paul Fearn/ Alamy Stock Photo p251 top; Photo 12/Alamy Stock Photo p235 left; Photo 12/Universal Images Group/ Getty Images p279 top; Pictorial Press Ltd/Alamy Stock Photo p215 top; Pictorial Press Ltd/Alamy Stock Photo p71, 87; Pictorial Press Ltd/Alamy Stock Photo p285 middle right; Private Collection/© Look and Learn / Bridgeman Images; p157; Private Collection/Bridgeman Images p116 left, 181 bottom right; Private Collection/Photo © Christie's Images/Bridgeman Images p217; Private Collection/Photo © Philip Mould Ltd, London/Bridgeman Images p177 top; Still Light/Alamy Stock Photo p77; Swim Ink 2/Corbis via Getty Images p207; Terry Parker/Mary Evans Picture Library p246; The Granger Collection/Alamy Stock Photo p173; The National Gallery, London/AKG Images p67 middle; The Print Collector/Alamy Stock Photo p219 top, 283 bottom; The Print Collector/Getty Images p209; Timewatch Images/Alamy Stock Photo p24; Towneley Hall Art Gallery and Museum, Burnley, Lancashire/Bridgeman Images p67 top; V&A Images/ Alamy Stock Photo p177 bottom; World History Archive/Alamy Stock Photo p99.

HarperCollins*Publishers*
1 London Bridge Street
London SE1 9GF
www.harpercollins.co.uk

First published by HarperCollins*Publishers* 2017

10 9 8 7 6 5 4 3 2
Text © Sara Sheridan with Daisy Goodwin 2017
A Mammoth Screen/Masterpiece Co-production for ITV
Television series, photographs and 'Victoria' logo © Mammoth Screen Limited 2017. All rights reserved.
Main *Victoria* series photography by Gareth Gatrell. Scotland unit photography Mark Mainz.
Cover photography © Gareth Gatrell
All other images © see page 303
Design © Smith & Gilmour

All quotes featured in margins are taken from the original fictional *Victoria* television scripts written
by Daisy Goodwin and may differ, in places, to the words spoken on screen.

Transcripts of Victoria's journals, containing all original stress and emphasis, can be found at
www.queenvictoriasjournals.org

While every effort has been made to trace the owners of copyright material reproduced herein and
secure permissions, the publishers would like to apologise for any omissions and will be pleased to
incorporate missing acknowledgements in any future edition of this book.

With thanks to Patrick Smith.

Sara Sheridan and Daisy Goodwin assert the moral right to be identified as the authors of this work

A catalogue record of this book is available from the British Library
ISBN: 978-0-00-825970-9
Printed and bound by GPS Group